ACTS AT YOUR
FINGERTIPS

MAMMALS

BROWN
BEAR
BOOKS

Published by Brown Bear Books Limited

An imprint of
The Brown Reference Group plc
68 Topstone Road
Redding
Connecticut
06896
USA
www.brownreference.com

ISBN-10: 1-933834-03-X
ISBN-13: 978-1-93383-403-0

Authors: Amy-Jane Beer and Pat Morris

Editorial Director: Lindsey Lowe

Project Director: Graham Bateman

Art Director: Steve McCurdy

Editor: Virginia Carter

Artists: Denys Ovenden, Priscilla Barrett, with Michael Long, Graham Allen, Malcolm McGregor, Rob van Assan

Printed in USA

Jacket artwork: Front: Denys Ovenden. Reverse: Rob van Assan.

Contents

Introduction

Mammals are the most advanced form of life to appear on this planet to date. They evolved from inconspicuous mammal-like reptiles that existed some 200 million years ago, when the dinosaurs were in their ascendancy. The first true mammals looked like today's solenodons and fed on insects that they caught at night.

Today there are about 4,680 species of mammals alive. About one-third are rodents (rats, mice, squirrels, and so on). And one in five is a bat. The smallest mammal is Kitti's hog-nosed bat, *Craseonycteris thonglongyai*, which weighs only about one-twentieth of an ounce (1.5 g), while the largest is the blue whale, *Balaenoptera musculus*, which weighs up to 130 tonnes or more.

As well as vast differences in size, mammals have varied lifestyles. The naked mole rat, *Heterocephalus glaber*, stays in a single burrow for its entire life, while some whales and seals travel over 10,000 miles (16,000 km) on annual migrations. Some mammals live solitary lives except when they meet to mate; others form vast colonies numbering thousands. Yet others live permanently in tightly organized social systems in which each individual knows its place. Some defend territory with sophisticated scent-marking and recognition systems. Some mammals have only one young at a time, often at intervals well in excess of a year, but mice and rabbits breed almost continuously. Some mammals can run

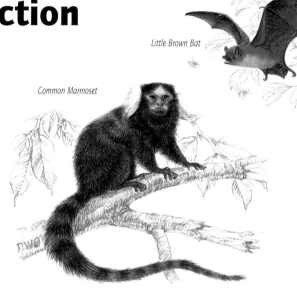

Little Brown Bat

Common Marmoset

very fast, but there are also swimmers, burrowers, gliders, and flyers. Mammals range from the poles to the tropics and from oceans, lakes, and rivers to deserts. They eat grass, flesh, fish, insects, fruit, bamboo, nectar, and gum. They shout, sing, and stay silent. Mammals are truly the world's most diverse and adaptable group. *Facts at Your Fingertips: Mammals* demonstrates this diversity.

What Makes a Mammal?

Mammals are often described as "warm-blooded"; the more correct term is endothermic. Reptiles and even some fish are also warm inside, but they cannot maintain a high blood temperature without basking in the sun or constantly moving around to generate heat from their muscles—they are ectothermic. Mammals (like birds) differ in that they generate heat internally, so their temperature is not only high but is kept constant at 95 to 100°F (35–38°C), depending on the species. The scientific term for such animals is homeothermic.

Mammal bodies are covered in hair (sometimes very sparsely). Hair traps a layer of air next to the skin, which insulates it from extremes of temperature around it. Mammals also sweat and lose heat as the moisture evaporates. Mammals also have a variety of shapes and sizes of teeth to suit their different diets. They are not the only animals to bear live young, but they are unique in that mothers produce milk, which means that the infants have no need to forage for food.

Rank	Scientific name	Common name
Phylum	Chordata	Animals with a backbone
Class	Mammalia	All mammals
Order	Carnivora	Flesh-eaters/carnivores
Family	Felidae	All cats
Genus	*Panthera*	Big cats
Species	*leo*	Lion

The kingdom Animalia is subdivided into phylum, classes, orders, families, genera, and species. Above is the classification of the lion.

Examples of the major groups of mammal.

Plains Zebra

Northern Elephant Seal

Bottlenose Dolphin

Black-Tailed Prairie Dog

American Black Bear

Black-Tailed Jack Rabbit

Short-Beaked Echidna

About this Book

Just by looking, we can see that lions, tigers, and the domestic cat are related, and that rats and mice are quite different from deer and antelope. Scientists take this study much further and to minute detail in the science of taxonomy, in which detailed relationships are worked out using a hierarchy of categories called taxa. Mammals all belong to the class Mammalia, which is divided into 27 orders. Examples include the order Carnivora (flesh-eating mammals such as lions, wolves, and otters) and Rodentia (rodents such as rats and mice). In *Facts at Your Fingertips: Mammals* you will find representatives of most mammal orders, which are color coded. Within an order such as Carnivora, for example, all catlike mammals are placed in the same family (Felidae), and doglike mammals in the family Canidae. Very closely related cats such as the lion and the tiger are grouped in the genus *Panthera*. Lions are

distinguished from, say, tigers by the scientific names *Panthera leo* and *Panthera tigris* respectively. In this book you will find illustrated entries on 112 species of mammals, grouped by order and family.

Each entry follows a fixed structure. The color-coded header strip denotes the order or groups of related orders to which each animal belongs and gives its common name. The fact panel then lists its scientific name and other taxonomic information followed by sections that describe different features of the animal and its lifestyle. Like all animals, the survival of many mammals is in doubt as they suffer from pressures brought to bear by humans. Under the heading "Status" information is given on the threats or lack of threat facing each animal. For definitions of the categories of threat see Glossary under IUCN and CITES. Finally, a world map visually portrays the distribution of each species, showing its natural range, unless otherwise indicated.

Lion

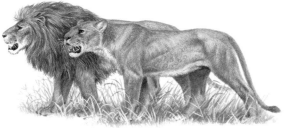

Common name Lion

Scientific name *Panthera leo*

Family Felidae

Order Carnivora

Size Length head/body: 5–8 ft (1.4–2.5 m); tail length: 27.5–41 in (70–105 cm); height at shoulder: 42–48 in (107–123 cm). Male 20–50% bigger than female

Weight 265–550 lb (120–250 kg)

Key features Huge, muscular cat with long, thin tail tipped with black tuft; body light buff to tawny brown; male develops thick mane of dark fur; head large with powerful, crushing jaws; eyes yellowish-brown

Habits Lives in prides; hunts alone and cooperatively; most active between dusk and dawn; rests up to 21 hours per day

Breeding One to 6 cubs (average 3–4) born after gestation period of 100–119 days. Weaned at 6–7 months; sexually mature at 3–4 years. May live up to 30 years in captivity, rarely more than 13 in the wild

Voice Variety of puffs, grunts, snarls, and roars

Diet Large mammal prey, including antelope, giraffe, zebra, hogs, and buffalo; also carrion

Habitat Savanna grasslands, open woodlands, desert margins, and scrub

Distribution Scattered populations in sub-Saharan Africa; population in Gir Forest, northwestern India

Status Population: several thousand; IUCN Vulnerable; CITES II. Asian lions fewer than 300; IUCN Endangered; CITES I. Declining outside protected areas

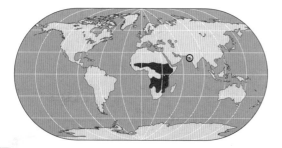

Tiger

Common name Tiger

Scientific name *Panthera tigris*

Family Felidae

Order Carnivora

Size Length head/body: 4.6–9 ft (1.4–2.7 m); tail length: 23–43 in (60–110 cm); height at shoulder: 31–43 in (80–110 cm)

Weight Male 200–660 lb (90–300 kg); female 143–364 lb (65–165 kg)

Key features Huge, highly muscular cat with large head and long tail; unmistakable orange coat with dark stripes; underside white

Habits Solitary and highly territorial; active mostly at night; climbs and swims well

Breeding Litters of 1–6 (usually 2 or 3) cubs born at any time of year after gestation period of 95–110 days. Weaned at 3–6 months; females sexually mature at 3–4 years, males at 4–5 years. May live up to 26 years in captivity, rarely more than 10 in the wild

Voice Purrs, grunts, and blood-curdling roars

Diet Mainly large, hooved mammals, including deer, buffalo, antelope, and gaur

Habitat Tropical forests and swamps; grasslands with good vegetation cover and water nearby

Distribution India, Bhutan, Bangladesh, Nepal; China; southeastern Siberia; Myanmar (Burma), Vietnam, Laos, Thailand, and Sumatra

Status Population: 5,000–7,500; IUCN Endangered; CITES I. Previously hunted for fur and body parts, and to protect people and livestock

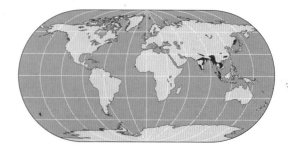

Cheetah

Common name Cheetah

Scientific name *Acinonyx jubatus*

Family Felidae

Order Carnivora

Size Length head/body: 44–59 in (112–150 cm); tail length: 24–31 in (60–80 cm); height at shoulder: 26–37 in (67–94 cm)

Weight 46–159 lb (21–72 kg)

Key features Very slender, long-limbed cat with small head, rounded ears, and long tail held in low sweep; fur pale gold to tawny, paler on belly with black spots; end of tail has dark bands

Habits Diurnal; can be solitary and nomadic or live in small groups

Breeding Litters of 1–8 (usually 3–5) cubs born at any time of year after gestation period of 90–95 days. Weaned at 3–6 months; sexually mature at 18 months but rarely breeds before 2 years. May live up to 19 years in captivity, up to 14 in the wild, but usually many fewer

Voice Purrs, yelps, moans, and snarls; also a high-pitched churring; females use birdlike chirping to reassure young

Diet Mostly gazelles and impalas; other hoofed animals depending on opportunity

Habitat Savanna grassland, scrub, and semidesert

Distribution Widespread but scattered populations throughout sub-Saharan Africa, excluding the Congo Basin. Small population in Iran

Status Population: fewer than 15,000; IUCN Vulnerable; CITES I. Range and population greatly reduced, now protected in most of its range

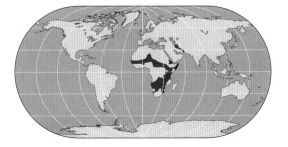

Leopard

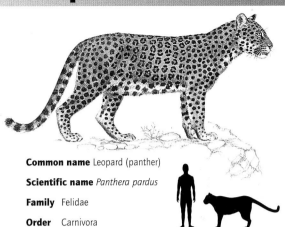

Common name Leopard (panther)

Scientific name *Panthera pardus*

Family Felidae

Order Carnivora

Size Length head/body: 35–75 in (90–190 cm); tail length: 23–43 in (58–110 cm); height at shoulder: 18–31 in (45–78 cm)

Weight Male 160–200 lb (73–90 kg); female 62–132 lb (28–60 kg)

Key features Large, lean cat with long tail; pale gold to tawny coat marked all over with black spots arranged into rosettes on back and flanks

Habits Solitary; mostly nocturnal; excellent climber

Breeding Litters of 1–6 (usually 2 or 3) young born after gestation period of 90–105 days during favorable season (varies throughout range). Weaned at 3 months; sexually mature at 3 years. May live over 20 years in captivity, probably well over 20 in the wild

Voice Rasping calls, grunts, and roars

Diet Mostly small- to medium-sized hoofed mammals; also monkeys, rabbits, rodents, and invertebrates, such as beetles

Habitat Varied; includes lowland forest, grassland, brush, and semidesert

Distribution Most of southern Asia and sub-Saharan Africa, excluding rain forests of Congo Basin. Small populations in North Africa, Middle East, Arabia, and China

Status Population: fewer than 700,000; IUCN Endangered and Critically Endangered (several subspecies); CITES I. Widespread but declining due to habitat loss and hunting

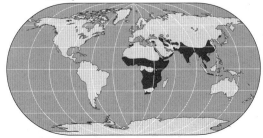

CARNIVORES
Bobcat

Common name Bobcat

Scientific name *Felis rufus*

Family Felidae

Order Carnivora

Size Length head/body: 25.5–41 in (65–105 cm); tail length: 4–7.5 in (11–19 cm); height at shoulder: 17.5–23 in (45–58 cm)

Weight 9–33 lb (4–15 kg)

Key features Small, slender-limbed, short-tailed cat; fur thick, varies in color from buff to brown with darker spots and streaks; ears pointed, often with tufts; ruff of fur around jowls

Habits Solitary; territorial; active day or night

Breeding Litters of 1–6 kittens born after gestation period of 60–70 days, usually in spring. Weaned at 2 months; females sexually mature at 1 year, males at 2 years. May live up to 32 years in captivity, probably no more than 13 in the wild

Voice Usually silent, but hisses and shrieks in distress and during courtship

Diet Small mammals and birds; sometimes larger prey, such as small deer; domestic animals

Habitat Varied; includes forests, scrub, swamp, mountains, and the edges of deserts

Distribution North America

Status Population: 700,000–1 million; CITES II. Declined in the past due to persecution; still harvested for fur under license in some states

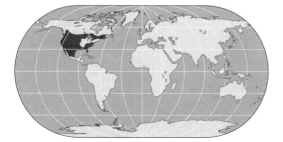

CARNIVORES
Puma

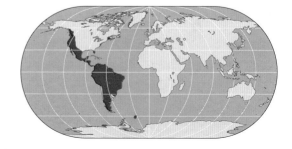

Common name Puma (cougar, panther, mountain lion, catamount)

Scientific name *Felis concolor*

Family Felidae

Order Carnivora

Size Length head/body: 38–77 in (96–196 cm); tail length: 21–32 in (53–82 cm); height at shoulder: 24–27.5 in (60–70 cm)

Weight Male 148–264 lb (67–120 kg); female 80–132 lb (36–60 kg)

Key features Large, muscular cat with long legs and tail; small head with large, rounded ears; coat color varies from silvery gray through warm buffy tones to dark tawny

Habits Solitary; active at any time of day; climbs extremely well

Breeding Litters of 1–6 (usually 3 or 4) kittens born January–June after gestation period of 90–96 days. Weaned at 3 months; sexually mature at 2.5–3 years. May live up to 21 years in captivity, rarely more than 14 in the wild

Voice Hisses, growls, whistles, and screams

Diet Carnivorous; mostly deer; also other hoofed animals, rodents, and hares

Habitat Very varied; lowland and mountain forests, swamps, grassland, and scrub

Distribution Most of North and South America

Status Population: many thousands in total, but Florida panther (*F. c. coryi*) fewer than 50; IUCN Critically Endangered (2 subspecies); CITES II (at least 2 subspecies). Persecuted as a pest in the past; now protected in parts of its range although still hunted in other areas

8

Gray Wolf

Common name Gray wolf (timber wolf)

Scientific name *Canis lupus*

Family Canidae

Order Carnivora

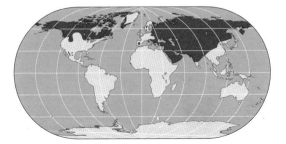

Size Length head/body: 35–56 in (89–142 cm); tail length: 12–20 in (30–51 cm); height at shoulder: 23–28 in (58–77 cm)

Weight 22–175 lb (10–80 kg). Male larger than female

Key features Large, long-legged dog with thick fur and bushy tail; fur usually gray, although color varies with distribution

Habits Social, although sometimes solitary; more or less nocturnal; hunts communally to bring down prey up to 10 times its own weight

Breeding One to 11 (average 6) pups born in a den after gestation period of 63 days. Weaned at 5 weeks; sexually mature at 2 years. May live up to 16 years in captivity, rarely more than 13 in the wild

Voice Growls, barks, whines, and howls

Diet Mainly large mammal prey, including deer, moose, muskox, mountain sheep, bison, beavers, and hares

Habitat Almost anywhere from tundra to scrub, grassland, mountains, and forest

Distribution Northern Hemisphere

Status Population: many thousands; IUCN Vulnerable; CITES I (India, Pakistan, Nepal, Bhutan); elsewhere CITES II. Now more stable following centuries of persecution

Coyote

Common name Coyote

Scientific name *Canis latrans*

Family Canidae

Order Carnivora

Size Length head/body: 30–39 in (76–100 cm); tail length: 12–19 in (30–48 cm); height at shoulder: about 24 in (60 cm)

Weight 15.5–44 lb (7–20 kg). Male slightly larger than female

Key features Typical wolf but smaller and slighter in build than gray wolf; ears large and pointed; muzzle narrow; fur shaggy and usually a shade of beige or gray; paler on belly, but darkening to black on tip of tail

Habits Mostly nocturnal, but can be active at any time of day; some migrate into mountains in summer; less social than gray wolf

Breeding Litters of 2–12 (average 6) born in spring after gestation period of 63 days. Weaned at 5–6 weeks; sexually mature at 1 or 2 years. May live up to 21 years in captivity, usually fewer than 15 in the wild

Voice Wide repertoire of barks, whines, and howls

Diet Carnivorous; mostly mammals, including rabbits, woodchucks, rodents, and deer; also carrion

Habitat Grasslands and prairie, scrub, and forest

Distribution North America

Status Population: abundant. Common and widespread; hunted for fur and as a pest

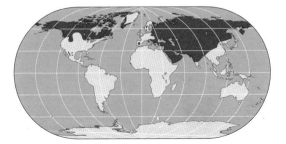

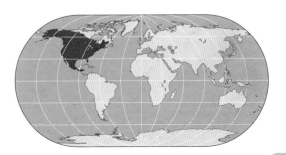

Red Fox

Common name
Red fox

Scientific name *Vulpes vulpes*

Family Canidae

Order Carnivora

Size Length head/body: 18–35.5 in (45–90 cm); tail length: 12–21.5 in (30–55 cm); height at shoulder: up to 14 in (36 cm)

Weight 7–31 lb (3–14 kg)

Key features Typical fox with long, narrow body ending in thick, brushy tail; pointed muzzle and ears; neat legs and feet; fur typically red, but varies from deep gold to dark brown, fading to white on muzzle, chest, and belly; often darker on legs; black and pale variants known

Habits Mostly nocturnal; sometimes lives in family groups, but usually hunts alone; nonbreeding males are solitary

Breeding Litters of 1–12 (usually 3–7) cubs born in spring after gestation period of 51–53 days. Weaned at 8–10 weeks; sexually mature at 10 months. May live up to 12 years in captivity, rarely more than 5 in the wild

Voice Barks, whines, yelps, screams, excited "gekkering" when playing

Diet Omnivorous; rodents and other small mammals; also insects, worms, and fruit

Habitat Diverse; includes farmland, forest, grassland, moorland, tundra, and urban areas

Distribution Europe and North America; also parts of Africa and Asia; introduced to Australia

Status Population: abundant. Persecuted as vermin; also hunted for sport

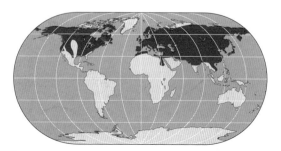

Arctic Fox

Common name Arctic fox

Scientific name *Vulpes (Alopex) lagopus*

Family Canidae

Order Carnivora

Size Length head/body: 18–27 in (46–68 cm); tail length: 12 in (30 cm); height at shoulder: 11 in (28 cm)

Weight 3–20 lb (1.4–9 kg)

Key features Stout-looking fox with short legs, long, bushy tail, small, rounded ears, and a thick, woolly coat; fur pure white in winter in high Arctic animals; fur extends to soles of feet

Habits Social; sometimes migratory; active at any time of day; does not hibernate

Breeding Litters of 6–12 (occasionally as many as 25) pups born in early summer after gestation period of 49–57 days. Weaned at 2–4 weeks; sexually mature at 10 months. May live up to 16 years in captivity, fewer in the wild

Voice Barks, whines, screams, and hisses

Diet Mainly carnivorous; prey includes seals, rodents (especially lemmings), seabirds, fish, invertebrates such as crabs, mollusks, and insects, and carrion; scavenges from kills made by other Arctic predators; occasionally plant material

Habitat Arctic and northern alpine tundra, boreal forest, ice cap, and even sea ice

Distribution Arctic regions of Canada, Alaska, Greenland, Iceland, Finland, Sweden, Norway, and Russia

Status Population: abundant. Generally common, although range and population size have declined recently. Protected in Norway, Sweden, and Finland; hunted for fur and as vermin elsewhere

African Wild Dog

Common name African wild dog (African hunting dog, painted hunting dog)

Scientific name *Lycaon pictus*

Family Canidae

Order Carnivora

Size Length head/body: 30–44 in (76–112 cm); tail length: 12–16 in (30–41 cm); height at shoulder: 24–31 in (61–78 cm)

Weight 37.5–80 lb (17–36 kg)

Key features Lean, long-legged dog with large ears and 4 toes on each foot (other dogs have 5 digits on front feet); fur is short, thin, and patterned with variable blotches and speckles of black, brown, yellow, and white; dark skin often shows through coat

Habits Highly social; active by day; packs wander widely except when breeding

Breeding Litters of up to 20 pups (usually 4–8) born at any time of year after gestation period of 79–80 days. Weaned at 11 weeks; sexually mature at 2 years. May live up to 17 years in captivity, 11 in the wild

Voice Excited squeaks and twitters; also hoots and wails that carry long distances

Diet Carnivorous, mostly taking hoofed mammals such as antelope

Habitat Savanna grassland and open woodland

Distribution Africa south of the Sahara

Status Population: probably fewer than 5,000 and declining; IUCN Endangered. Protected by law in most of its range

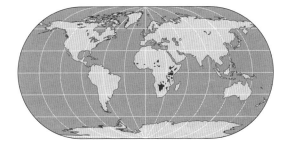

Dingo

Common name Dingo

Scientific name *Canis dingo (C. lupus dingo)*

Family Canidae

Order Carnivora

Size Length head/body: 34–48 in (86–122 cm); tail length: 10–15 in (26–38 cm); height at shoulder: 17–25 in (44–63 cm)

Weight 22–53 lb (10–24 kg)

Key features Large robust-looking dog; sandy fur with pale markings on feet, chest, muzzle, and tail tip; long muzzle and pricked ears; bushy tail

Habits Lives in packs of up to 12, defending common territory; hunts alone or in packs

Breeding One to 10 (average 5) pups born in underground den during winter after gestation period of 63 days. Weaned at 3 months; sexually mature at 2 years. May live a little over 14 years in captivity, up to 14 in the wild

Voice Typical doglike bark, whines, yelps, and howls

Diet Varies according to prey available; anything from kangaroos and rabbits to insects and carrion

Habitat Diverse; hot deserts, tropical and temperate forests, mountains, scrub, and ranch land

Distribution Australia, New Guinea, Indochina, Indonesia, Borneo, and Philippines

Status Population: abundant. Declining in numbers, but not included in any conservation programs because most countries do not protect introduced or alien species

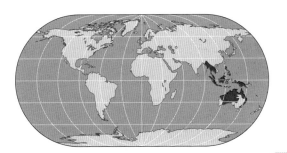

Polar Bear

Common name Polar bear

Scientific name *Ursus maritimus*

Family Ursidae

Order Carnivora

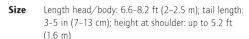

Size Length head/body: 6.6-8.2 ft (2-2.5 m); tail length: 3-5 in (7-13 cm); height at shoulder: up to 5.2 ft (1.6 m)

Weight Male 660-1,760 lb (300-800 kg); female 330-660 lb (50-300 kg)

Key features Huge bear with thick, off-white coat; head relatively small; feet large and furry

Habits Solitary; migratory and partially nomadic; pregnant females hibernate in winter; excellent swimmer

Breeding Litters of 1-4 tiny cubs born in midwinter after gestation period of 195-265 days (includes variable period of delayed implantation). Weaned from 6 months; sexually mature at 5-6 years. May live up to 45 years in captivity, 30 in the wild

Voice Grunts and growls

Diet Carnivorous: mainly seals but occasionally other animals such as reindeer; also fish, seabirds, carrion, and plant material in summer

Habitat Sea ice, ice cap, and tundra; equally at home in water and on land

Distribution Arctic Circle; parts of Canada, Alaska, Russia, Scandinavia, and Greenland

Status Population: 20,000-30,000; IUCN Lower Risk: conservation dependent; CITES II. Main threat is from human exploitation of Arctic habitats

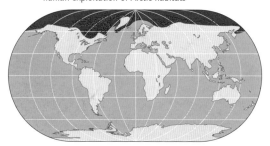

American Black Bear

Common name American black bear

Scientific name *Ursus americanus*

Family Ursidae

Order Carnivora

Size Length head/body: 4.9-5.9 ft (1.5-1.8 m); tail length: 4.5 in (12 cm); height at shoulder: up to 36 in (91 cm)

Weight Male 250-600 lb (113-272 kg); female 200-310 lb (91-141 kg)

Key features Large bear with thick, but not shaggy coat; fur can be variety of colors, but usually brown or black; muzzle less furry than rest of face

Habits Solitary; most active at night; swims and climbs well; hibernates over winter

Breeding Litters of 1-5 (usually 2 or 3) cubs born after gestation period of 220 days (including about 150 days delayed implantation). Weaned at 6-8 months; females sexually mature at 4-5 years, males at 5-6 years. May live up to 31 years in captivity, 26 in the wild

Voice Various grunts, rumbling growls, and woofing sounds; cubs give high-pitched howls

Diet Mostly plant material, including fruit, nuts, grass, bark, and roots; fish; invertebrates such as insects and their larvae and worms; also honey, other mammals, and carrion

Habitat Forest and scrub; occasionally open spaces

Distribution Canada, Alaska, and U.S. south to Mexico

Status Population: 400,000-500,000; CITES II. Still common, but population now reduced due to hunting, persecution, and habitat loss

Brown Bear

Common name Brown bear (grizzly bear, big brown bear)

Scientific name *Ursus arctos*

Family Ursidae

Order Carnivora

Size Length head/body:
5.5–9.3 ft (1.7–2.8 m); tail length: 2.5–8 in (6–20 cm);
height at shoulder: 35–60 in (90–150 cm). Male bigger
than female

Weight 132–1,750 lb (60–800 kg)

Key features Medium to large bear with shaggy, light-brown to
black fur, often grizzled (grayish) on back and shoulders;
narrow snout; broad face

Habits Solitary; nonterritorial; hibernates over winter

Breeding Litters of 1–4 (usually 2) cubs born January–March
after gestation period of 180–266 days. Weaned at 5
months; sexually mature at 4–6 years. May live up to 40
years in captivity, 25 in the wild

Voice Various grunts and growls

Diet Mostly plant material, including grass, roots, and fungi;
also small invertebrates, fish, and carrion

Habitat Varied; tundra, open plains, alpine grassland, forests,
and wooded areas

Distribution Western Canada, Alaska, and northwestern U.S.;
northern Asia south of Arctic Circle; Scandinavia, eastern
Europe, and Middle East; Pyrenees, Alps, and Abruzzi
Mountains

Status Population: 220,000; CITES I (several Eurasian
subspecies); CITES II (North American subspecies).
Declining, but now more stable

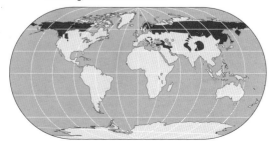

Giant Panda

Common name Giant panda
(panda, panda bear)

Scientific name
Ailuropoda melanoleuca

Family Ursidae

Order Carnivora

Size Length head/body: 47–59 in
(120–150 cm); tail length: 5 in
(13 cm); height at shoulder: up to 27.5–31 in
(70–80 cm)

Weight 165–350 lb (75–160 kg)

Key features Unmistakable large, furry bear with black legs,
shoulder band, eye patches, and ears; body is off-white

Habits Solitary; nonterritorial; active between dusk and dawn;
climbs well

Breeding One or 2 cubs born August–September after gestation
period of 97–163 days (includes variable period of
delayed implantation). Weaned at 8–9 months;
sexually mature at 6–7 years. May live up to 34 years
in captivity, fewer in the wild

Voice Varied sounds, including growls, moans, barks, squeaks,
and bleats

Diet Omnivorous, but mostly bamboo and some other plant
material; occasionally small animals

Habitat Mountainside forests with bamboo thickets at altitudes
of 3,300–13,000 ft (1,000–3,900 m)

Distribution Small remaining range in central China

Status Population: about 1,000; IUCN Endangered; CITES I. Has
declined greatly in range and population due to
hunting, habitat loss, and specialized lifestyle

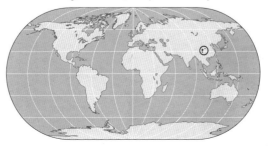

Spotted Hyena

Common name Spotted hyena

Scientific name *Crocuta crocuta*

Family Hyaenidae

Order Carnivora

Size Length head/body: 39-71 in (100-180 cm); tail length: 10-14 in (25-36 cm); height at shoulder: 28-35 in (70-90 cm)

Weight 88-200 lb (40-91 kg); female generally about 12% heavier than male

Key features Doglike, powerfully built animal with short tail and sloping back; pale sandy gray coat with dark, irregular blotches

Habits Usually nocturnal, but will venture out during the daytime; lives in clans

Breeding Usually 2, but up to 4 cubs born after gestation period of 4 months. Weaned at 8-18 months; sexually mature at 2 years. May live to over 40 years in captivity, probably fewer in the wild

Voice Loud whooping noises; crazy-sounding giggle

Diet Meat from carcasses killed by other predators; slow animals like waterbuck; also tortoises, fish, insects, and garbage

Habitat Acacia savannas; urban fringes

Distribution Africa south of Sahara, except for areas of thick forest; absent from most of South Africa

Status Population: several thousand; IUCN Lower Risk: conservation dependent. Widespread and fairly common, but disappearing from many places being unpopular with farmers

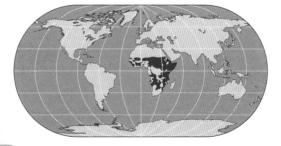

Common Raccoon

Common name Common raccoon

Scientific name *Procyon lotor*

Family Procyonidae

Order Carnivora

Size Length head/body: 18-27 in (45-68 cm); tail length: 8-12 in (20-30 cm); height at shoulder: about 10-12 in (25-30 cm). Male about 25% larger than female

Weight 11-18 lb (5-8 kg), but sometimes up to 33 lb (15 kg)

Key features Black "bandit" face mask, accentuated by gray bars above and below; black eyes; short, rounded ears; bushy tail with alternate brown and black rings (usually 5); body hairs long and gray

Habits Nocturnal; mainly solitary, although related females may live close to one another

Breeding Four to 6 young born around February to April after gestation period of 63 days. Weaned at 7 weeks; females usually sexually mature by their first spring, males by 2 years. May live over 17 years in captivity, up to 16 in the wild

Voice Chitters, purrs, hisses, barks, growls, snarls, and squeaks

Diet Fruit, berries, nuts, and seeds; fish, crayfish, clams, snails, and earthworms; crops such as corn and stored grain

Habitat Almost anywhere in North America, including urban areas

Distribution Southern Canada, U.S., and Central America

Status Population: abundant. Most common member of raccoon family; continues to expand its range and increase in numbers

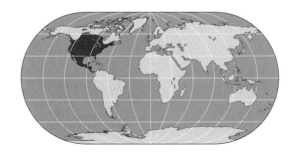

Least Weasel

Common name Least weasel (European common weasel)

Scientific name *Mustela nivalis*

Family Mustelidae

Order Carnivora

Size Length head/ body: 7-10 in (17-25 cm); tail length: 1-5 in (3-12 cm)

Weight 1.7-3 oz (48-85 g)

Key features Long, sleek body with short legs and short tail; flat, narrow head; fur reddish-brown in summer, with creamy-white neck and belly; turns white in winter in northern populations

Habits Solitary, territorial animals; fierce predators; very active both day and night all year round

Breeding Up to 2 litters of 1-9 young born each year after gestation period of 34-37 days. Weaned at 3-4 weeks; females sexually mature at 4 months, males at 8 months. May live up to 10 years in captivity, usually under a year in the wild

Voice Low trill to signal a friendly meeting between a male and a female; loud, harsh chirp or screech when disturbed or ready to attack

Diet Mainly small rodents, especially mice; also rabbits, lemmings, moles, pikas, birds, fish, lizards, and insects

Habitat Almost anywhere providing suitable cover and access to rodents, including meadows, farmlands, prairies, marshes, and woodlands

Distribution Northern Hemisphere: Canada, Alaska, Siberia, Japan, northern U.S., northern Europe, and Russia

Status Population: abundant. One of the more numerous small carnivores

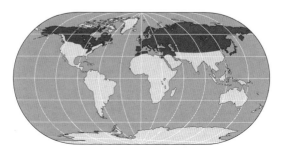

American Mink

Common name American mink

Scientific name *Mustela vison*

Family Mustelidae

Order Carnivora

Size Length head/body: 12-18.5 in (30-47 cm); tail length: 5-9 in (13-23 cm)

Weight 1.9-4 lb (0.9-1.8 kg); female 1-1.8 lb (0.5-0.8 kg)

Key features Resembles short-legged, glossy black or dark-brown cat; pointed muzzle

Habits Mainly nocturnal; swims and dives; uses burrows and lairs among tree roots at water's edge, also rabbit burrows, but does not dig for itself

Breeding One litter of 4-6 young born April-May after gestation period of 39-78 days, including a variable period of delayed implantation. Weaned at 5-6 weeks; sexually mature at 2 years. May live for 10 years in captivity, 2-3 in the wild

Voice Hisses when threatened; may scream defiantly in self-defense, but usually silent

Diet Fish, frogs, small mammals, waterside birds and their eggs; also some invertebrates such as beetles and worms, especially along coasts

Habitat Mostly lowland areas beside rivers, lakes, and ponds; also marshland and along seashores

Distribution Canada; eastern and most of central U.S.; introduced to Europe: in Britain, France, Italy, Spain, Ireland, Scandinavia, and Iceland

Status Population: abundant. Increasing in Europe

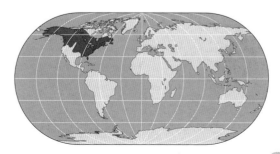

Wolverine

Common name Wolverine (glutton, skunk bear)

Scientific name *Gulo gulo*

Family Mustelidae

Order Carnivora

Size Length head/body: 24-26 in (62-67 cm); tail length: 5-10 in (13-25 cm); height at shoulder: 14-17 in (35-43 cm)

Weight 20-65 lb (9-29 kg). Male at least 10% bigger than female

Key features Low, thickset animal with short legs and large, powerful paws; coat dark brown but paler on face and flanks; tail thick and bushy

Habits Solitary creature that roams widely; mainly nocturnal in summer

Breeding One litter of up to 4 babies born February-March after gestation period of 30-40 days (including up to 9 months delayed implantation). Weaned at 8-10 weeks; sexually mature at 2-3 years. May live up to 18 years in captivity, 11 in the wild

Voice Hisses and growls when annoyed; also playful squeaks and grunts

Diet Mostly rodents; sometimes larger mammals, especially as carrion; also fruit, berries, birds, and eggs

Habitat Mountainous forests, rocky areas, and tundra in summer

Distribution Widely distributed across northern Europe and Russia; also Canada and northern U.S.

Status Population: unknown, probably low thousands; IUCN Vulnerable

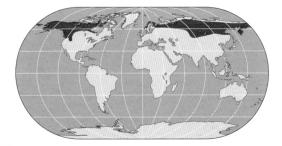

European Otter

Common name European otter

Scientific name *Lutra lutra*

Family Mustelidae

Order Carnivora

Size Length head/body: 24-35 in (60-90 cm); tail length: 14-18.5 in (35-47 cm); height at shoulder: about 6 in (15 cm). Male about 20% bigger than female

Weight 13-37 lb (6-17 kg)

Key features Long, slender body with short legs and long, tapering tail; light- or dark-brown fur with broad, flattened head, small ears, and small eyes; all 4 feet are webbed

Habits Lives alone; swims and dives well but can be active on land; usually nocturnal, may come out during the day

Breeding Usually 2-3 cubs born after gestation period of 2 months; births at any time of year in western Europe, more seasonal in the north and east. Weaned at 4 months; sexually mature at 1 year. May live up to 15 years in captivity, about 3-4 in the wild

Voice Occasional shrill whistle, otherwise silent

Diet Slow-swimming fish, especially eels, but also mussels, shrimps, crabs, and lobsters

Habitat Edges of rivers and lakes, often in reed beds; rocky coasts in some areas

Distribution From Britain throughout most of western Europe east to China and Japan; also in south India, Sri Lanka, Malaysia, Sumatra, and parts of North Africa

Status Population: widespread but scarce; IUCN Vulnerable; CITES I. Declining in most areas; has become extinct in parts of Europe in the last 50 years

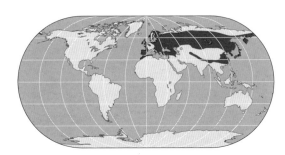

Sea Otter

Common name Sea otter

Scientific name *Enhydra lutris*

Family Mustelidae

Order Carnivora

Size Length head/body: 29.5-35 in (75-90 cm); tail length: 11-12.5 in (28-32 cm); height at shoulder: 8-10 in (20-25 cm)

Weight 30-85 lb (14-38 kg)

Key features Dark-brown otter with blunt-looking head that turns pale cream with age; feet completely webbed; hind feet form flippers

Habits Floats on back in kelp beds and calm waters; dives to feed from seabed

Breeding One pup born each year in early summer after gestation period of 4 months (including up to 8 months delayed implantation). Weaned at 5 months; females sexually mature at 3 years; males at 5-6 years, but do not breed successfully until at least 7 years. May live for over 20 years in captivity, similar in the wild

Voice Normally silent

Diet Crabs, shellfish, sea urchins, fish; other marine animals

Habitat Kelp beds and rocky seashores

Distribution Formerly along coasts across eastern and northern Pacific from California to Kamchatka and northern Japan; exterminated over most of its range, now reintroduced to coasts of California, Alaska, Oregon, and Washington

Status Population: about 150,000 and growing; IUCN Endangered; CITES II. Given full legal protection in 1911 and probably now secure

reintroduced population
in North America

European Badger

Common name European badger

Scientific name *Meles meles*

Family Mustelidae

Order Carnivora

Size Length head/body: 27.5-31 in (70-80 cm); tail length: 5-7 in (12-19 cm); height at shoulder: 12 in (30 cm)

Weight 18-26 lb (8-12 kg)

Key features Dog-sized animal with short legs and long, coarse hair, grizzled gray on back and black on belly; face is white with prominent black stripes running backward through the eyes

Habits Nocturnal; occupies a clan territory; often inactive for long periods in winter, but does not hibernate

Breeding Usually 1-4 cubs born around February after gestation period of 10-12 months (including 8-10 months delayed implantation). Weaned at about 4 months; sexually mature at 2 years. May live to be 16 years in captivity, 10 in the wild

Voice Occasional yelps and loud whickering noises

Diet Almost anything edible found at ground level, including worms, small mammals, roots, fruit, acorns, and beetles

Habitat Woodlands, farmlands, even suburban areas where there is access to food; prefers well-drained soils on slopes for burrowing

Distribution Widespread in most of Europe from Britain and Spain eastward to China and Japan

Status Population: probably at least 1.5 million. Generally scarce, even extinct in some areas, but increasingly common in parts of Britain

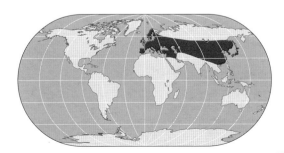

Striped Skunk

Common name Striped skunk

Scientific name *Mephitis mephitis*

Family Mustelidae

Order Carnivora

Size Length head/body: 12.5-18 in (32-45 cm); tail length: 7-10 in (17-25 cm); height at shoulder: 4 in (10 cm). Male larger, but female has longer tail

Weight 3-13 lb (1.5-6 kg)

Key features Cat-sized animal, with small head tapering to a bulbous nose; black coat with forked white stripes on back; white patch and stripe on head; long, bushy tail

Habits Mainly active at night and at dusk and dawn; generally solitary; squirts foul-smelling liquid when threatened; may swim if necessary

Breeding Three to 9 young born May–June after gestation period of 62-66 days (including delayed implantation). Weaned at 6-8 weeks; sexually mature at 1 year. May live 8-10 years in captivity, fewer than 3 in the wild

Voice Low growls, grunts, and snarls; also churring and short squeals; occasional screech or hiss

Diet Mainly insects; also small rodents, rabbits, birds, eggs, carrion, fruit, vegetables, and garbage

Habitat Forest or field edges, patches of brush, rocky outcrops, and wooded ravines; town gardens

Distribution Southern Canada, U.S., and northern Mexico

Status Population: abundant

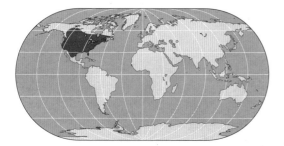

Meerkat

Common name Meerkat (suricate, gray meerkat, slender-tailed meerkat)

Scientific name *Suricata suricatta*

Family Herpestidae

Order Carnivora

Size Length head/body: 12-18 in (30-45 cm); tail length: 6-12 in (15-30 cm); height at shoulder: 4 in (10 cm)

Weight 3.3-5 lb (1.5-2.3 kg)

Key features Slender, short-legged animal; tan to gray with broken brown bands on back and sides; black eye rings, ears, and tail tip

Habits Social: lives in colonies of up to 30, but usually 10-15, animals; sentries posted to watch for predators while colony is foraging

Breeding Two to 5 young born after gestation period of 75 days. Weaned at 9-10 weeks; sexually mature at about 12 months. May live 13 years in captivity, up to 10 in the wild, but more commonly 6

Voice A variety of chirrups, trills, growls, and barks

Diet Insects, scorpions, and grubs; occasionally lizards, small snakes, birds, and mice

Habitat Dry savanna, open plains, and scrubland

Distribution Southern Africa in Angola, Namibia, South Africa, and southern Botswana

Status Population: abundant. Not threatened, but numbers have fallen in some areas

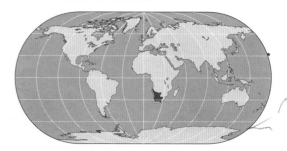

Northern Fur Seal

Common name Northern fur seal

Scientific name *Callorhinus ursinus*

Family Otariidae

Order Pinnipedia

Size Length: male up to 6.5 ft (2 m); female 3.7–4.6 ft (1.1–1.4 m)

Weight Male 300–615 lb (136–279 kg); female 66–110 lb (30–50 kg)

Key features Large fur seal; bulls reddish-brown and black, cows pale and more gray

Habits Spends most of the year swimming and diving out at sea; comes ashore to breed in early summer in large colonies

Breeding One young born per year after gestation period of 12 months (including 4 months delayed implantation). Weaned at 3–4 months; females sexually mature at 4 years, males at 6 years but rarely breed before 10 years. May live more than 30 years in captivity, 26 in the wild

Voice Loud bellowing and barking

Diet Mainly fish

Habitat Open sea within 60 miles (100 km) of the coast; comes ashore only to breed

Distribution North Pacific coasts as far south as California; main breeding colonies occur on Pribilof and Commander Islands

Status Population: about 1 million; IUCN Vulnerable

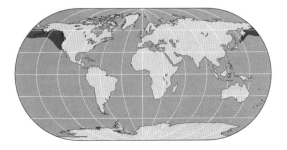

Walrus

Common name Walrus

Scientific name *Odobenus rosmarus*

Family Odobenidae

Order Pinnipedia

Size Length: male 8.8–11.5 ft (2.7–3.5 m); female 7.4–10.2 ft (2.3–3.1 m)

Weight Male 1,760–3,750 lb (800–1,700 kg); female 880–2,750 lb (400–1,247 kg)

Key features Vast, ponderous seal; generally pale brown all over; broad, deep snout bears 2 long tusks

Habits Feeds by diving in shallow seas; spends much time hauled out on shore, generally with other walruses

Breeding Single pup born April–June every 2 years after gestation period of more than 1 year. Weaned at up to 2 years; females sexually mature at 6–7 years, males at 8–10 years. May live over 40 years in the wild

Voice Bellowing and grunts; sometimes whistles

Diet Mollusks, crabs, worms, and invertebrates taken from seabed; occasionally fish

Habitat Arctic waters along edge of pack ice

Distribution Arctic Ocean: Pacific population along coasts of Siberia and Alaska, Atlantic population mainly around northern Canada, Greenland, and parts of Arctic Scandinavia

Status Population: at least 200,000 (Pacific); about 30–35,000 (Atlantic)

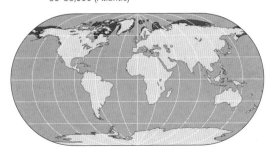

SEALS AND SEA LIONS

Northern Elephant Seal

Common name Northern elephant seal

Scientific name *Mirounga angustirostris*

Family Phocidae

Order Pinnipedia

Size Length: male 13-16.5 ft (4-5 m); female 6.5-10 ft (2-3 m)

Weight Male 2-3 tons (1.8-2.7 tonnes); female 1,300-2,000 lb (600-900 kg)

Key features Huge seal with bent, floppy nose; unlike almost all other seals, brown all over

Habits Spends most of its time at sea; occasionally hauls out to rest on rocky islands and beaches

Breeding Single pup born after gestation period of 11 months (including 2-3 months delayed implantation). Weaned at 4 weeks; females sexually mature at about 5 years, males at 8-9 years. May live up to 20 years, but males usually fewer than 12

Voice Bellows and roars

Diet Mostly squid caught in midwater; also some small sharks and slow-moving fish

Habitat Cold coastal waters

Distribution North Pacific coasts of North America from California to northern Mexico

Status Population: about 100,000-150,000

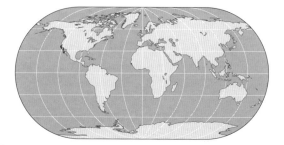

SEALS AND SEA LIONS

Gray Seal

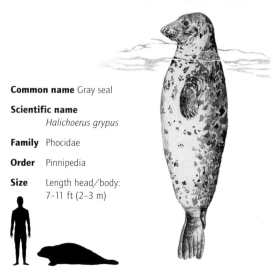

Common name Gray seal

Scientific name *Halichoerus grypus*

Family Phocidae

Order Pinnipedia

Size Length head/body: 7-11 ft (2-3 m)

Weight Male 375-680 lb (170-308 kg); female 230-410 lb (104-186 kg)

Key features Big, dark-gray seal with pale blotches; top of head forms flat profile; snout broad and conical in bull

Habits Spends most of year out at sea, but comes ashore to rest and breed; dives to catch food

Breeding Single calf born after gestation period of 11.5 months (including 3 months delayed implantation). Weaned at 3 weeks; females sexually mature at 4-5 years, males at 6-8 years. Females may live over 40 years, males many fewer, about 15-20 years

Voice Loud barking sounds

Diet Fish, especially cod and salmon; occasionally octopus

Habitat Rocky coasts with sandy beaches; open sea

Distribution Coasts of Britain, Scandinavia, Iceland, and Baltic; off Labrador and Nova Scotia (Canada), occasionally south as far as New Jersey

Status Population: about 200,000; IUCN Endangered (Baltic population)

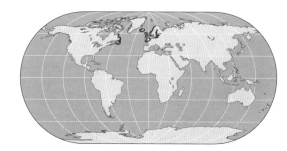

Killer Whale

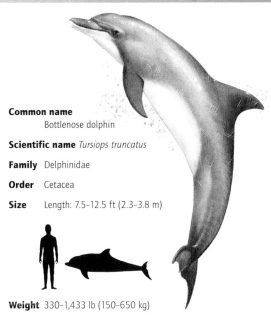

Common name
Killer whale (orca)

Scientific name *Orcinus orca*

Family Delphinidae

Order Cetacea

Size Length: male 17–29.5 ft (5.2–9 m);
female 15–25.5 ft (4.5–7.7 m)

Weight 3–10 tons (2.5–9 tonnes)

Key features Striking black-and-white markings;
body mainly black with white patch
behind eye, white cheeks and belly, and gray saddle
patch; head rounded with no obvious snout; tall,
triangular dorsal fin, up to 6 ft (1.8 m) high in male;
broad, rounded flippers; tail black on top, white on
underside

Habits Social, living in a tight-knit family group or "pod"; fast,
active swimmer; acrobatic at the surface, will breach,
spy-hop, and tail slap

Breeding Single calf born about every 8 years after gestation
period of 17 months. Weaned at 14–18 months; sexually
mature at 12–16 years. Males may live 35–60 years,
females up to 90 years in the wild; rarely survives more
than a few years in captivity

Voice Varied, including complex, often pulsed, calls

Diet Small fish and squid to seals, turtles, seabirds, and even
other whales

Habitat Open sea to coastal waters; estuaries; often around ice
floes in polar waters

Distribution Every ocean in the world, from polar regions to
equator

Status Population: 100,000; IUCN Lower Risk: conservation
dependent; CITES II. Widespread and quite numerous

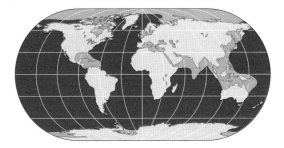

Bottlenose Dolphin

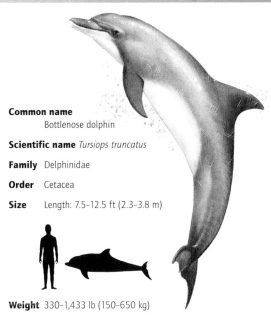

Common name
Bottlenose dolphin

Scientific name *Tursiops truncatus*

Family Delphinidae

Order Cetacea

Size Length: 7.5–12.5 ft (2.3–3.8 m)

Weight 330–1,433 lb (150–650 kg)

Key features Robust dolphin with a wide head and body and
rounded forehead; body mostly gray with a lighter or
white underside; color patterns are variable

Habits Active, social dolphin usually seen in groups

Breeding Single calf born every 4–5 years after gestation period
of 1 year. Weaned at 4–5 years; females sexually mature
at 5–12 years, males at 10–12 years. May live up to 50
years in the wild, fewer in captivity

Voice High-pitched whistles and clicks

Diet Large variety of food, including fish, squid, octopus,
cuttlefish, and mollusks

Habitat Wide range of habitats from open water to harbors,
bays, lagoons, estuaries, and rocky reefs

Distribution Widespread in temperate and tropical waters

Status Population: unknown, perhaps hundreds of thousands of
individuals; CITES II. A common species, especially in
particular areas

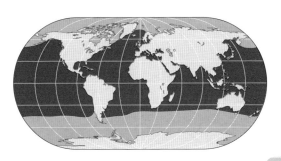

Beluga

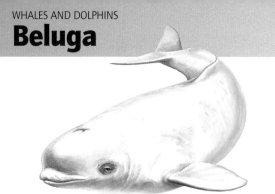

Common name Beluga (white whale)

Scientific name *Delphinapterus leucas*

Family Monodontidae

Order Cetacea

Size Length: 10-16 ft (3-5 m). Male larger than female

Weight 1,100-3,300 lb (500-1,500 kg)

Key features Stocky, white-colored whale; no dorsal fin; head small and rounded; flippers broad, short, paddle shaped, and highly mobile; tail fluke frequently asymmetrical

Habits Social animals, rarely seen alone; masculine groups of 3-15, nursery groups of mature females and several young of various ages; during migrations congregations of hundreds or even thousands may be seen

Breeding One calf born every 3 years after gestation period of 14-14.5 months. Weaned at 20-24 months; females sexually mature at 5 years, males at 8 years. May live 30-40 years in the wild, some have been known to live to 50 years; does not survive so long in captivity

Voice Trills, moos, clicks, squeaks, and twitters; sometimes called "sea canary"

Diet Mostly bottom feeders, eating fish, crustaceans, worms, and mollusks

Habitat Coastal and offshore in cold waters, usually near ice; shallow waters, rivers, and estuaries

Distribution Coasts of Arctic regions of North America, Greenland, northern Russia, and Svalbard

Status Population: about 100,000; IUCN Vulnerable; CITES II

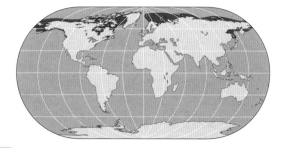

Sperm Whale

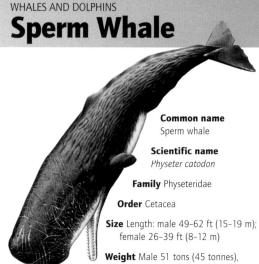

Common name Sperm whale

Scientific name *Physeter catodon*

Family Physeteridae

Order Cetacea

Size Length: male 49-62 ft (15-19 m); female 26-39 ft (8-12 m)

Weight Male 51 tons (45 tonnes), maximum 65 tons (57 tonnes); female 17 tons (15 tonnes), maximum 27 tons (24 tonnes)

Key features Largest toothed whale; dark-gray to dark-brown skin with white patches on belly; skin has a wrinkled appearance; often scarred; large, square-ended head; dorsal fin reduced to a small, triangular hump; short, paddle-shaped flippers

Habits Females and young live in breeding schools, young males in bachelor schools, both with 20-25 individuals; older males solitary or in small groups; join breeding schools to mate

Breeding Single calf born every 4-6 years after gestation period of 14-16 months. Weaned at 1-3 years, sometimes longer; females sexually mature at 7-13 years, males at 18-21 years. May live at least 60-70 years

Voice Clicks used for communication and echolocation

Diet Mostly squid; also cuttle, octopus, and fish

Habitat Deep waters, often near the continental shelf; females and calves stay in warm waters, males migrate to colder feeding grounds

Distribution Found in all the oceans of the world

Status Population: estimates vary from 200,000 (minimum) to 1.5 million (maximum); IUCN Vulnerable; CITES I

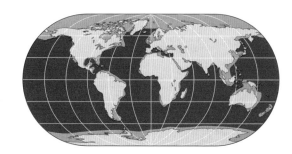

Gray Whale

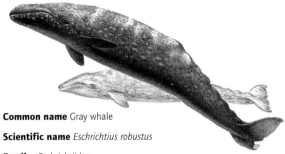

Common name Gray whale

Scientific name *Eschrichtius robustus*

Family Eschrichtiidae

Order Cetacea

Size Length: male 39–46 ft (12–14 m); female 43–49 ft (13–15 m)

Weight 26–40 tons (22.5–35 tonnes)

Key features Robust baleen whale; fairly short, upwardly curved head; skin mottled gray, covered with patches of barnacles and whale lice; no dorsal fin, but low hump followed by series of bumps running to the large tail flukes; flippers small and paddle shaped

Habits Generally found in small groups of 1–3, but larger groups of up to 16 sometimes seen; large gatherings form at feeding and breeding grounds; performs one of the longest migrations of any mammal

Breeding Single calf born about every 2 years after gestation period of 12–13 months. Weaned at 7–8 months; sexually mature at between 5 and 11 years. May live 50–60 years, maximum documented 77 years

Voice Rumbles, groans, whistles, rasps, chirps, moans, growls, and bongs

Diet Small invertebrates scooped off the seabed, including crustaceans, mollusks, and worms

Habitat Shallow, coastal waters

Distribution Pacific Ocean; main population migrates between summer feeding grounds north of Alaska in Chukchi and Bering seas and winter breeding grounds off Baja California; smaller population found off Korea and Japan, but this group is close to extinction

Status Population: 20–25,000; IUCN Lower Risk: conservation dependent; Critically Endangered (northwestern Pacific stock); CITES I. Fairly common off western U.S.

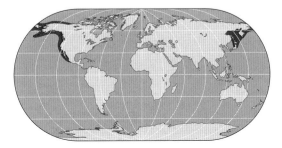

Humpback Whale

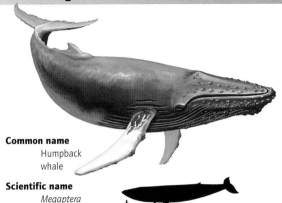

Common name Humpback whale

Scientific name *Megaptera novaeangliae*

Family Balaenopteridae

Order Cetacea

Size Length: male 38–50 ft (11.5–15 m). Male generally slightly smaller than female

Weight About 34 tons (30 tonnes); up to 55 tons (48 tonnes)

Key features Large, stocky baleen whale; upper body black or blue-black, underside white; long flippers; head and front edge of flippers have raised lumps called tubercles; tail flukes different in every individual

Habits More social than other rorqual whales, rarely seen alone; congregates in large groups to feed and breed; moves individually or in small parties of 2–3 within groups

Breeding One calf usually produced every 2 years after gestation period of 11–12 months. Weaned at 11 months; sexually mature at 4–6 years. May live 40–50 years, occasionally over 70

Voice Complex underwater songs consisting of grunts, groans, rasps, twitters, and moos

Diet Seasonal feeders on krill (shrimplike crustaceans) and small fish

Habitat Oceanic; enters shallow tropical waters in winter for breeding

Distribution Widely distributed; occurs seasonally in all oceans and from the Arctic to Antarctic

Status Population 30,000; IUCN Vulnerable; CITES I. Uncommon and threatened

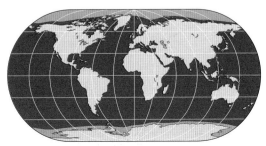

West Indian Manatee

Common name West Indian manatee (Caribbean manatee)

Scientific name *Trichechus manatus*

Family Trichechidae

Order Sirenia

Size Length: 12–15 ft (3.7–4.6 m)

Weight Up to 1.4 tons (1.2 tonnes)

Key features Large, sluggish, and slow-moving creature; grayish-brown in color, with paddle-shaped tail and no hind limbs; skin naked with patches of green algae and a few scattered, bristly hairs; blunt-ended head with thick, fleshy lips and small, piggy eyes

Habits Moves slowly, floating and diving in shallow water; often found in small family groups

Breeding Single young born after gestation period of about 1 year, with long intervals between births. Weaned at 2 years; sexually mature at 8 years. May live at least 28 years, probably considerably longer

Voice Normally silent

Diet Aquatic plants, floating and submerged; also grass and other vegetation overhanging from riverbanks

Habitat Estuaries, large rivers, and shallow seas

Distribution Florida, Caribbean, and coastal waters of South America as far as Brazil

Status Population: probably about 10,000–12,000; IUCN Vulnerable; CITES I

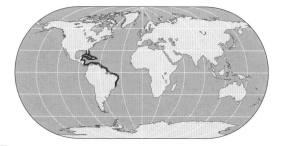

Dugong

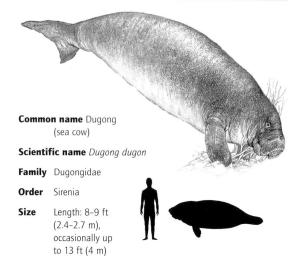

Common name Dugong (sea cow)

Scientific name *Dugong dugon*

Family Dugongidae

Order Sirenia

Size Length: 8–9 ft (2.4–2.7 m), occasionally up to 13 ft (4 m)

Weight 300–800 lb (136–360 kg), occasionally up to 2,000 lb (900 kg)

Key features Large seal- or whalelike mammal with gray, almost hairless skin; front flippers bent at an angle part way along; small eyes and large upper lip with tough, bristly pads; flat, crescent-shaped tail; no hind limbs

Habits Floats lazily in shallow water, diving occasionally to eat plants from seabed; usually seen singly or in small groups

Breeding Single young born at intervals of 3–7 years (twins rare) after gestation period of 13–14 months. Young first graze at 3 months, weaned at 18 months; sexually mature at 9–10 years. May live over 70 years

Voice Generally silent, but occasional chirps and whistles

Diet Mostly sea grasses; sometimes green or brown seaweeds

Habitat Shallow seas along tropical coasts

Distribution Indian Ocean and southwestern Pacific up to 27° north and south of equator

Status Population: probably fewer than 150,000 spread over a huge area; IUCN Vulnerable; CITES Australian population II; elsewhere I

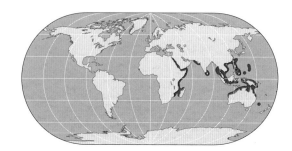

Demidoff's Bush Baby

Common name
Demidoff's bush baby (Demidoff's dwarf galago)

Scientific name *Galagoides demidoff*

Family Galagonidae

Order Primates

Size Length head/body: 3–6 in (7–15 cm); tail length: 8–10 in (20–26 cm)

Weight 1.5–3.4 oz (43–96 g)

Key features Gray-black to reddish coat with paler yellowish underparts; white stripe between eyes and down bridge of nose; pointed, upturned nose and relatively short ears

Habits Nocturnal; lively: runs along branches and leaps in tree canopy; sleeps in hollow trees, dense vegetation, or in nests; females may sleep in huddles of 10 or more; forages alone

Breeding Usually 1 young, sometimes 2, born per year after gestation period of 110–114 days. Weaned at 2 months; sexually mature at 8–9 months. May live 12 or more years in captivity, probably fewer in the wild

Voice Series of loud chirps, increasing to a crescendo; buzzing alarm call

Diet Insects: mainly beetles, moths, caterpillars, and crickets; also gum (tree sap) and some fruit

Habitat Dense secondary growth; forest edges or land running along the sides of roads

Distribution Equatorial western and central Africa

Status Population: relatively abundant; CITES II. Numerous in places, although not often seen

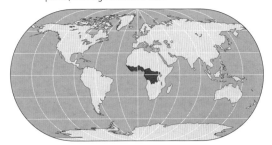

Ringtailed Lemur

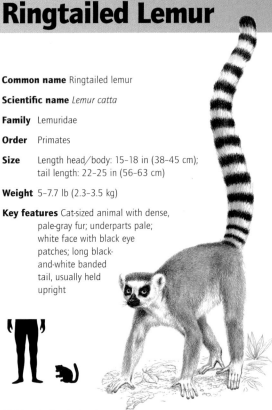

Common name Ringtailed lemur

Scientific name *Lemur catta*

Family Lemuridae

Order Primates

Size Length head/body: 15–18 in (38–45 cm); tail length: 22–25 in (56–63 cm)

Weight 5–7.7 lb (2.3–3.5 kg)

Key features Cat-sized animal with dense, pale-gray fur; underparts pale; white face with black eye patches; long black-and-white banded tail, usually held upright

Habits Active during the day; feeds in trees but also spends a lot of time on the ground

Breeding Single infant (occasionally twins) born between August and November after gestation period of approximately 136 days. Weaned at 4 months; sexually mature at 2 or 3 years. May live over 30 years in captivity, fewer in the wild

Voice Catlike mews, grunts, yaps, howls, and purrs

Diet Mainly fruit; also leaves, bark, and sap

Habitat Dry deciduous scrub and forest

Distribution South and southwestern Madagascar

Status Population: fewer than 100,000; IUCN Endangered; CITES II. Declining due to loss of habitat

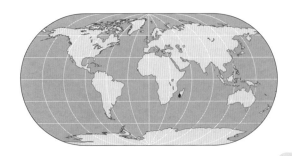

Common Marmoset

Common name Common marmoset

Scientific name Callithrix jacchus

Family Callitrichidae

Order Primates

Size Length head/body: 4.7–6 in (12–15 cm); tail length: 12–14 in (30–35 cm)

Weight 10.5–12.7 oz (300–360 g)

Key features Mottled gray-brown coat; crown blackish with white patch on forehead; long white ear tufts; gray-and-white banded tail

Habits Diurnal; lives in stable groups of up to 15 animals

Breeding One to 4 young (often twins) born twice yearly after gestation period of 130–150 days. Weaned at 100 days; males sexually mature at 11–15 months, females at 14–24 months. May live 16 years in captivity, 10 in the wild

Voice Soft "phee" contact call; angry chatter and high-pitched whistle as a warning call

Diet Tree sap, insects, spiders, fruit, flowers, and nectar; also lizards, frogs, eggs, and nestlings

Habitat Atlantic coast forest and gallery forest along rivers; forest patches in dry thorn scrub and bush savanna

Distribution Northeastern Brazil west and south from the Rio Parnaiba

Status Population: abundant; CITES I. Relatively common and widespread; not seriously threatened

Squirrel Monkey

Common name Squirrel monkey (common squirrel monkey)

Scientific name Saimiri sciureus

Family Cebidae

Order Primates

Size Length head/body: 11–14.5 in (28–37 cm); tail length: 14.5–18 in (37–45 cm)

Weight 19–44 oz (550–1,250 g)

Key features Small olive-green monkey with orange hands and white around the face; muzzle black

Habits Active by day in groups of 30–40 animals

Breeding Single young born once a year after gestation period of 170 days. Weaned at about 1 year; females sexually mature at 3 years, males at 5 years. May live up to 30 years in captivity, probably fewer in the wild

Voice Variety of squeaks, chirps, and purring noises

Diet Mainly fruit and insects

Habitat Forests, including mangroves from sea level to 6,500 ft (2,000 m)

Distribution Tropical South America

Status Population: abundant; CITES II. Common animal. Large numbers previously captured for the pet trade, now protected in the wild and no longer threatened by such activities

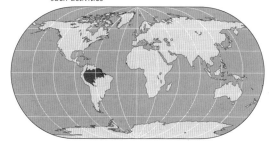

Brown Howler Monkey

Common name Brown howler monkey

Scientific name *Alouatta fusca*

Family Cebidae

Order Primates

Size Length head/body: 18–23 in (45–58 cm); tail length: 20–26 in (50–66 cm). Male generally larger than female

Weight 9–16 lb (4–7 kg)

Key features Thickset monkey, with swollen throat region in adult males; coat dark reddish brown, paler below

Habits Tree dwelling; lives in small groups; active mainly during daylight hours

Breeding Single young born each year after gestation period of about 189 days. Weaned at about 10–12 months; females sexually mature at 3–4 years, males take longer. May live to about 20 years in captivity, 15 in the wild

Voice Very loud howling and roars made especially by males

Diet Mainly leaves, but also fruit

Habitat Tropical forests

Distribution Coastal forests of southeastern Brazil

Status Population: unknown, probably low thousands; IUCN Vulnerable; CITES II. Threatened by destruction and fragmentation of forest habitat

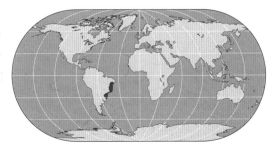

Proboscis Monkey

Common name Proboscis monkey

Scientific name *Nasalis larvatus*

Family Cercopithecidae

Order Primates

Size Length head/body: male 24–30 in (60–76 cm); female 21–24 in (53–60 cm); tail length: 22–24 in (56–60 cm)

Weight Male 35–55 lb (16–25 kg); female 15–24 lb (7–11 kg)

Key features Long, dangling nose in adult males, less developed in females

Habits Mainly active in late afternoon to dark; lives in small social groups

Breeding Single young born at any time of year after gestation period of 106 days. Weaned at 7 months; sexually mature at about 3 years. May live up to 23 years in captivity, usually fewer in the wild

Voice Males make a long, drawn-out resonant honk; female call is a milder sound, similar to that of a goose

Diet Mainly leaves, but fruit and flowers also eaten when available

Habitat Found near fresh water in lowland rain forests or mangrove swamps

Distribution Borneo and Mentawai Islands in the Malay Archipelago

Status Population: probably fewer than 250,000; IUCN Vulnerable; CITES I. Habitat destruction is threatening populations; hunting is also on the increase

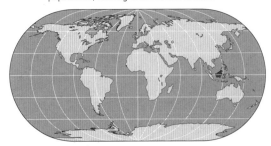

Hanuman Langur

Savanna Baboon

Common name
Hanuman langur

Scientific name
Semnopithecus entellus

Family Cercopithecidae

Order Primates

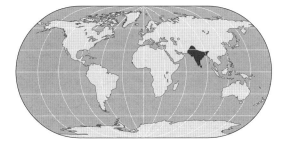

Size Length head/body: 16–31 in (41–78 cm); tail length: 27–42.5 in (69–108 cm)

Weight Male 20–66 lb (9–30 kg); female 16.5–40 lb (7.5–18 kg)

Key features Slender, agile monkey; long tail; upperparts gray, brown, or buff; crown and underparts white or yellowish; black face, ears, hands, and feet; prominent brow ridge

Habits Active by day in small social groups dominated by 1 or more males; forages on ground as well as in trees

Breeding Usually a single offspring born after gestation period of 190–210 days. Weaned at 10–12 months; females sexually mature at 3–4 years, males at 6–7 years. May live about 25 years in captivity, 15 in the wild

Voice Resonant whoops and guttural alarm calls

Diet Mainly leaves; also some fruits, seeds, flowers, and sometimes crops

Habitat Varied: includes wet tropical forests, shrubs, desert edges, alpine scrub, and urban areas

Distribution From Pakistan through Himalayas to Nepal and Bangladesh; India and Sri Lanka

Status Population: probably about half a million; Indian population estimated at 233,800 (1986); IUCN Lower Risk: near threatened; CITES I

Common name Savanna baboon (yellow baboon)

Scientific name *Papio cynocephalus*

Family Cercopithecidae

Order Primates

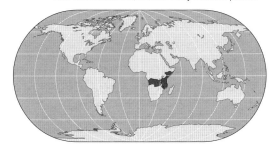

Size Length head/body: male 31–45 in (79–114 cm); female 20–28 in (51–71 cm); tail length: 18–27 in (46–68 cm)

Weight Male 48–66 lb (22–30 kg); female 24–33 lb (11–15 kg)

Key features Coat yellowish-gray; shiny black patch of bare skin over buttocks; eyes set close together with prominent brow-ridge above; long, ridged muzzle; powerful jaws with long canine teeth in adult males

Habits Active during the day; forages on the ground and in trees; lives in large troops averaging 30–40 members

Breeding Usually single baby born every 1–2 years after gestation period of 6 months. Weaned at 1 year; females sexually mature at 5 years, males at 7 years. May live up to 40 years in captivity, 20–30 in the wild

Voice Barks, grunts, screeches, yelps, and clicks

Diet Grass, fruit, seeds, bulbs, lichen, mushrooms, insects, young ungulates, and crops

Habitat Savanna grassland, open woodland and forest edge, rocky hill country, and semidesert with some grass and thorn bush

Distribution Widespread in central and eastern Africa

Status Population: unknown—tens of thousands; IUCN Lower Risk: near threatened; CITES II. Fairly common primate

B rb ry M c que

Common name Barbary macaque (Barbary ape)

Scientific name *Macaca sylvanus*

Family Cercopithecidae

Order Primates

Size Length head/body: 22–30 in (55–76 cm). Female about 20% smaller than male

Weight 10–20 lb (4.5–9 kg)

Key features Grayish-brown monkey with almost no tail; face hairless with large cheek pouches to store food

Habits Lives in small groups of up to about 40 animals (usually fewer); spends more time on the ground than other macaques; active during the day

Breeding Single young born at any time of year after gestation period of 210 days. Weaned at about 1 year; females sexually mature at 2–4 years, males at 5–7 years. May live up to about 30 years in captivity, about 20 in the wild

Voice Wide range of typical monkey sounds

Diet Mostly plant material, including fruit and leaves, seeds, shoots, acorns, tubers, bark, and pine needles; some animal food such as insects (especially caterpillars)

Habitat Rocky mountain slopes and montane woodland

Distribution Morocco, Algeria, Tunisia, and Gibraltar

Status Population: about 15,000; IUCN Vulnerable; CITES II. Once found widely across North Africa, but now reduced to a few scattered populations

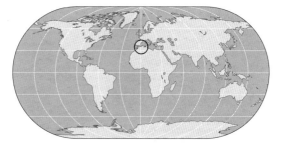

J p nese M c que

Common name Japanese macaque (snow monkey)

Scientific name *Macaca fuscata*

Family Cercopithecidae

Order Primates

Size Length head/body: 18.5–24 in (47–60 cm); tail length: 3–5 in (7–12 cm)

Weight Male 22–40 lb (10–18 kg); female 15.5–26.5 lb (7–12 kg)

Key features Thick, brown to gray coat; bare, red-colored face and buttocks; short tail

Habits Active by day; highly social: lives in troops averaging 20–30 animals, but sometimes up to 100; forages on ground and in trees

Breeding Single infant born every 2 years (usually between May and September) after gestation period of 5–6 months. Weaned at 6 months; females sexually mature at 3–4 years, but usually first breed at 6, males sexually mature at 5–6 years. May live up to about 30 years in captivity, similar in the wild

Voice Various long- and short-distance calls

Diet Fruit, insects, young leaves, and small animals; sometimes raids crops

Habitat Upland and mountain broad-leaved forest

Distribution Japan

Status Population: about 35,000–50,000 (1990); IUCN previously Endangered, temporarily listed as Data Deficient (2000); CITES II. Listed as Threatened by U.S. Endangered Species Act, but status in wild disputed

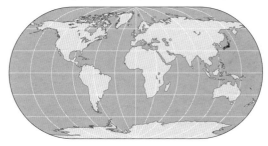

Chimpanzee

Common name Chimpanzee

Scientific name *Pan troglodytes*

Family Hominidae

Order Primates

Size Length head/body: male 27.5–35 in (70–89 cm); female 25–33 in (63–84 cm); height: 39–66 in (99–168 cm)

Weight Male 75–154 lb (34–70 kg); female 57–110 lb (26–50 kg)

Key features Coat brownish or black, graying with age; face bare and brownish pink

Habits Diurnal; nights spent in platform nests in trees; usually travels on ground and seen in groups; sometimes walks upright, but usually on all fours using knuckles of hands

Breeding Single young born every 5 or 6 years after gestation period of about 230 days. Weaned at 3.5–4.5 years; sexually mature at around 7 years, but females do not breed until aged 14–15, males at 15–16 years. May live up to 60 years in captivity, similar in the wild

Voice Wide range of calls, including hoots, barks, grunts, and screams

Diet Varied; includes fruit, flowers, seeds, bark, insects, birds' eggs, and meat

Habitat Deciduous, montane, and tropical rain forests; also patchy savanna woodland

Distribution Western and central Africa

Status Population: 150–230,000; IUCN Vulnerable; CITES I. Threatened due to deforestation

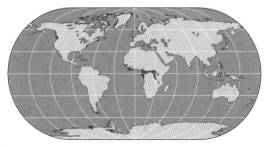

Western Lowland Gorilla

Common name Western lowland gorilla

Scientific name *Gorilla gorilla gorilla*

Family Hominidae

Order Primates

Size Height: male about 5.5 ft (1.7 m), occasionally to 5.9 ft (1.8 m); female 5 ft (1.5 m); arm span: 7.5 ft (2.3 m)

Weight Male 310–450 lb (140–204 kg); female 200 lb (90 kg)

Key features Largest primate; bulky body; arms longer than legs; coat relatively short and brown to dark gray; mature males have silver-gray back; broad face with fairly small jaws

Habits Lives in small groups of 4 to 8 animals, with 1 dominant "silverback" male; active during the day, nights spent in nests; docile, spends around a third of the day resting

Breeding Usually 1 young born every 4 years after gestation period of 250–270 days. Weaned at 2.5–3 years; females sexually mature at 6–8 years, males at 8–10 years. May live 50 years in captivity, 35 in the wild

Voice Roars, growls, barks, grunts, purrs, croaks, hoots, squeaks, and screeches

Diet Fruit, seeds, leaves, plant stems, bark, and invertebrates such as termites and caterpillars

Habitat Swamp and tropical forest

Distribution Central-western Africa

Status Population: fewer than 50,000; IUCN Endangered; CITES I. Vulnerable to poaching and habitat loss

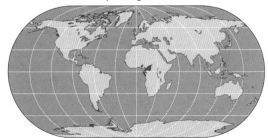

Mountain Gorilla

Common name Mountain gorilla (eastern gorilla)

Scientific name *Gorilla beringei beringei*

Family Hominidae

Order Primates

Size Height (upright): male 4.6–5.9 ft (1.4–1.8 m); female 4.3–5 ft (1.3–1.5 m); arm span: 7.5 ft (2.3 m)

Weight Male up to 400 lb (181 kg); female up to 200 lb (90 kg)

Key features Large, bulky ape with barrel-shaped body; arms muscular, longer than legs; coat blue-black, turning gray with age, males with silver patch on back; hair short on back, long elsewhere; broad face and massive jaws

Habits Social groups of 5–30 animals centered around 1 dominant "silverback" male; docile, mostly feeds or rests; males display strength by chest-beating

Breeding Usually 1 baby born every 4 years after 250–270 days' gestation. Weaned at 2.5–3 years; female sexually mature at 8–10 years, male at 10. May live 35 years

Voice Howling, roaring, grunting, and snarling

Diet Leaves, stems, berries, roots, pulp, and bark

Habitat Montane rain forest and subalpine scrub at altitudes of 5,400–12,400 ft (1,645–3,780 m)

Distribution Borders of Democratic Republic of Congo, Rwanda, and Uganda

Status Population: about 320; IUCN Critically Endangered; CITES I. Most threatened gorilla species

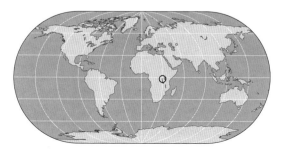

Orangutans

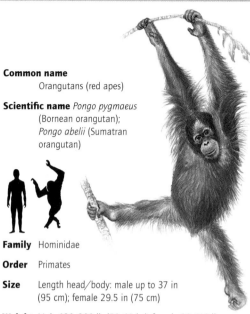

Common name Orangutans (red apes)

Scientific name *Pongo pygmaeus* (Bornean orangutan); *Pongo abelii* (Sumatran orangutan)

Family Hominidae

Order Primates

Size Length head/body: male up to 37 in (95 cm); female 29.5 in (75 cm)

Weight Male 130–200 lb (59–91 kg); female 88–110 lb (40–50 kg)

Key features Very long arms; feet are handlike; coat sparse and coarse, ranging from orange to dark brown

Habits Solitary; spends most of its time in treetops; active during the day, rests overnight in nests among branches

Breeding Single young born about every 8 years after gestation period of 8 months. Weaned at about 3 years; females sexually mature at 12 years, males at 15 years. May live 60 years in captivity, 45–50 in the wild

Voice Males make loud resonant calls with the help of their large throat pouches at a volume comparable to that of a lion's roar

Diet Fruit (such as mangoes and figs), young shoots, bark, and insects

Habitat Lowland and hilly tropical rain forest

Distribution Confined to the islands of Sumatra (Indonesia) and lowland Borneo

Status Population: about 20,000; IUCN Endangered; CITES I. Forest clearance is biggest threat

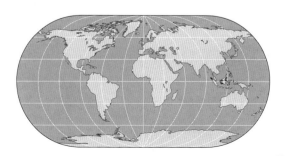

African Elephant

Common name African elephant

Scientific name *Loxodonta africana*

Family Elephantidae

Order Proboscidea

Size Length head/body (including trunk): 20-25 ft (6-7.5 m); tail length: 40-60 in (100-150 cm); height at shoulder: male 10.8 ft (3.3 m); female 8.9 ft (2.7 m).

Weight Male up to 6.8 tons (6 tonnes); female up to 3.4 tons (3 tonnes)

Key features Gray body; large head and ears; long ivory tusks; flexible trunk; skin with sparsely scattered black, bristly hairs; flat forehead and back; 4 toes on front feet, 3 on hind feet

Habits Females live in family groups of typically 2 or 3 sisters, plus offspring

Breeding Usually 1 calf born every 3-4 years in wet season after gestation period of 656 days. Weaned at 6 years; female sexually mature at 10 years, male at 25-30 years. May live more than 70 years in captivity, 60 in the wild

Voice "Trumpeting," rumbles or "purring," roars, snorts, squeals, screams, and low growls

Diet Grasses, tree leaves and fruit, bark

Habitat Mainly savanna grassland

Distribution Eastern and central Africa south of the Sahara

Status Population: fewer than 600,000; IUCN Endangered; CITES I in most countries, II in Botswana, Namibia, and Zimbabwe. Declining species

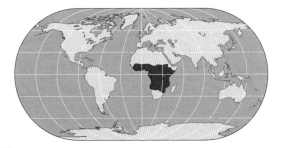

Rock Hyrax

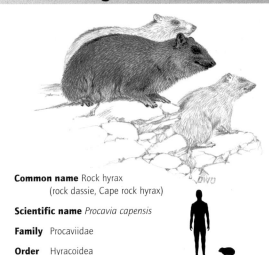

Common name Rock hyrax (rock dassie, Cape rock hyrax)

Scientific name *Procavia capensis*

Family Procaviidae

Order Hyracoidea

Size Length head/body: 12-23 in (30-58 cm)

Weight 6.6-8.8 lb (3-4 kg)

Key features Rotund body with short legs and no tail; small head with pointed snout, long whiskers, and round ears; fur dense, but coarse and a variable shade of brownish-gray, fading to creamy white on underside

Habits Diurnal; basks in sun; social; nimble and fast moving; can be aggressive

Breeding Single litter of 1-6 young born in wet season (summer and fall, different in Northern and Southern Hemispheres) after gestation period of 7-8 months. Weaned at 1 month but may suckle for up to 5, sexually mature at 16-17 months. May live up to 11 years in captivity, 8 in the wild

Voice Various squeals, whistles, and chattering sounds

Diet Wide variety of plant material

Habitat Rough scrub and hillsides with plenty of rocky outcrops and crevices

Distribution Africa and the Middle East south of a line from Senegal in West Africa to Turkey

Status Population: abundant

White Rhinoceros

Common name White rhinoceros (square-lipped rhinoceros, grass rhinoceros)

Scientific name *Ceratotherium simum*

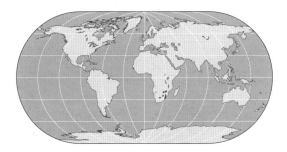

Family Rhinocerotidae

Order Perissodactyla

Size Length head/body: 11–14 ft (3.3–4.2 m); tail length: 20–27.5 in (50–70 cm); height at shoulder: 5–6 ft (1.5–1.8 m). Male 20–90% bigger than female

Weight 1.9–2.6 tons (1.7–2.3 tonnes)

Key features Huge gray-brown rhino with large head, 2 horns, and very square upper lip

Habits Active by day and night; dominant males solitary and territorial; wallows in mud or water; generally shy and docile

Breeding Single calf born after gestation period of 16 months. Weaned at 12–14 months; sexually mature at 5 years, but males not dominant enough to breed until 10–12 years. May live up to 50 years in captivity, similar in the wild

Voice Varied repertoire of grunts, snorts, chirps, squeals, growls, bellows, and pants

Diet Grass

Habitat Flat, lightly forested plains close to water

Distribution Reserves and national parks in southern Africa and Democratic Republic of Congo

Status Population: 7,500; IUCN Lower Risk: conservation dependent, Critically Endangered (northern subspecies); CITES I

Plains Zebra

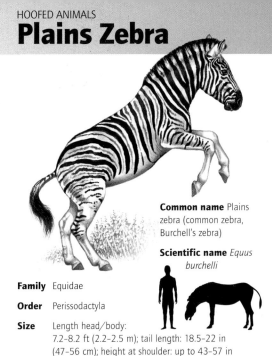

Common name Plains zebra (common zebra, Burchell's zebra)

Scientific name *Equus burchelli*

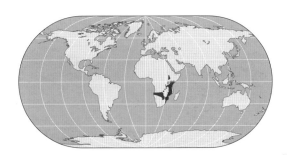

Family Equidae

Order Perissodactyla

Size Length head/body: 7.2–8.2 ft (2.2–2.5 m); tail length: 18.5–22 in (47–56 cm); height at shoulder: up to 43–57 in (110–145 cm)

Weight 385–710 lb (175–322 kg)

Key features Deep-bodied, short-legged zebra; thick, erect mane; black stripes broader than in other species, especially on rump, and do not always extend onto belly and legs; stripes sometimes interspersed with pale-brown lines

Habits Social: lives in nonterritorial, single-male harems or bachelor groups; active day and night

Breeding Single young born after gestation period of 360–396 days. Weaned at 7–11 months; females sexually mature at 16–22 months, males from 4 years. May live up to 40 years in captivity, usually many fewer in the wild

Voice Typical horse calls; snorts, gasps, squeals

Diet Mostly grass; some shrubs and flowering plants; shoots, twigs, and leaves of trees

Habitat Savanna and lightly wooded or scrubby grassland

Distribution Southern and eastern Africa outside forested and developed land

Status Population: 750,000; IUCN Data Deficient. Declining; protected in several national parks

Brazilian Tapir

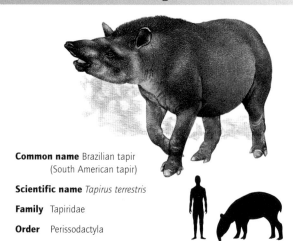

Common name Brazilian tapir (South American tapir)

Scientific name *Tapirus terrestris*

Family Tapiridae

Order Perissodactyla

Size Length head/body: up to 7.2 ft (2.2 m); tail length: 3 in (8 cm); height at shoulder: 30–42 in (77–108 cm)

Weight Up to 550 lb (250 kg)

Key features Bulky animal with narrow front end, rounded rump, slender legs, and short tail; head tapers to short snout; ears oval and erect, eyes small; coat sparse with narrow mane; 4 toes on front feet, 3 on hind feet

Habits Mainly nocturnal; solitary and aggressive to other tapirs, but nonterritorial; swims and dives well; wallows in mud

Breeding Single young (occasionally twins) born after gestation period of 13 months. Weaned at about 12 months; sexually mature at 2–3 years. May live up to 35 years in captivity, probably many fewer in the wild

Voice Loud squeals, low-frequency clicks and whistling sounds

Diet Mainly grass, leaves, and shoots of terrestrial and aquatic plants; also twigs, bark, and fruit; sometimes raids crops such as rice and corn

Habitat Humid forest with dense vegetation and permanent sources of water

Distribution Northern and central South America east of Andes

Status Population: probably several thousand; IUCN Lower Risk: near threatened; CITES II. Declining due to habitat loss and hunting

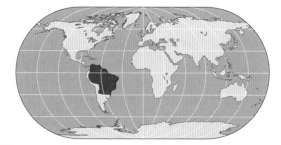

Common Hippopotamus

Common name Common hippopotamus (hippo)

Scientific name *Hippopotamus amphibius*

Family Hippopotamidae

Order Artiodactyla

Size Length head/body: 10.8–11.3 ft (3.3–3.5 m); tail length: 14–20 in (35–50 cm); height at shoulder: 4.6 ft (1.4 m)

Weight Male 1.4–2.8 tons (1.3–2.5 tonnes); female 1.2 tons (1 tonne)

Key features Bulky body with broad, expanded muzzle; skin naked and gray-brown to blue-black on upper body; lower parts pinkish; 4-toed feet; lower canine teeth enlarged as tusks

Habits Mostly nocturnal; rests in water by day, grazes on savanna grassland by night

Breeding One calf born, usually in water, after gestation period of about 240 days. Weaned at 6–8 months; females sexually mature at 7–15 years, males at 6–13 years. May live about 49 years in captivity, 45 in the wild

Voice Squeals, honks, bellows, deep rumbles; loud "ho-ho-ho"

Diet Savanna grasses, but some commercial crops (mainly rice) taken in agricultural regions

Habitat Short grasslands; rivers, lakes, and muddy wallows

Distribution West, central, East, and southern Africa

Status Population: 174,000; IUCN Vulnerable (subspecies *H. a. tschadensis*); CITES II. Species as a whole not currently threatened, although numbers are declining

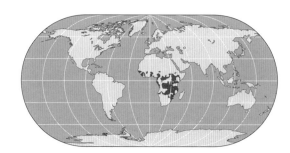

Warthog

Common name Warthog

Scientific name *Phacochoerus africanus*

Family Suidae

Order Artiodactyla

Size Length head/body: 43–53 in (110–135 cm); tail length: 16 in (40 cm); height at shoulder: 22–34 in (55–85 cm)

Weight 110–220 lb (50–100 kg)

Key features Relatively long-legged, short-necked pig; prominent curved tusks and facial warts; tough snout for unearthing food; gray skin nearly naked with sparse black hairs on body and paler bristles around the jaws

Habits Generally active throughout day, sleeps in burrows at night; social: closely related females form clans; males join clans during breeding season, but are otherwise solitary

Breeding Two to 3 (but up to 8) piglets born after gestation period of 170–175 days. Weaned at 6 months; sexually mature at 1.5 years. May live up to 18 years in the wild, not usually kept in captivity

Voice Grunts, squeals, and growls; males make mumbling noises during courtship

Diet Grass, roots, berries, bark of young trees, and occasionally other animal remains

Habitat Usually dry, open wooded areas

Distribution African savannas

Status Population: abundant; IUCN Endangered (subspecies *P. a. aeliani*). Eliminated from areas of intensive farming; elsewhere abundant, especially in national parks

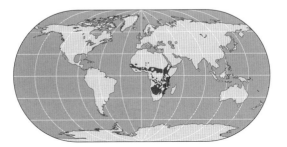

Dromedary Camel

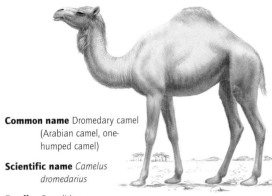

Common name Dromedary camel (Arabian camel, one-humped camel)

Scientific name *Camelus dromedarius*

Family Camelidae

Order Artiodactyla

Size Length head/body: 7.5–11.4 ft (2.3–3.5 m); tail length: 14–21 in (35–55 cm); height to top of hump: 5.9–7.5 ft (1.8–2.3 m)

Weight 660–1,540 lb (300–698 kg)

Key features Tall; long neck and legs; single large dorsal hump; tail thin and hairy; head small, with small, furry ears, large, thickly lashed eyes, closable nostrils, and split upper lip; fur short and woolly, pale beige to dark brown

Habits Active during the day in small herds; not territorial and generally nonaggressive

Breeding Single calf (twins rare) born every other year at most at any time of year after gestation period of 15 months (births peak in the rainy season). Weaned at 12–18 months; females sexually mature at 3 years; males take 6 years to reach size at which they can defend mates. May live up to 50 years in captivity, similar in the wild

Voice Rumbling moans and grunts

Diet Any desert plant, including those with high salt content

Habitat Deserts

Distribution Originally from Arabian Peninsula; feral and semiwild populations also in North Africa, Asia, and central Australia

Status Population: may exceed 19 million; IUCN Extinct in the Wild. Domesticated

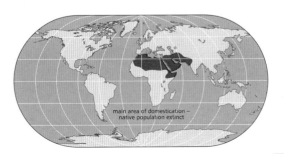

main area of domestication – native population extinct

Llama

Common name
Llama

Scientific name *Lama glama*

Family Camelidae

Order Artiodactyla

Size Length head/body: 47–88 in (120–225 cm); tail length: 6–10 in (15–25 cm); height at shoulder: up to 43–47 in (109–119 cm)

Weight 286–342 lb (130–155 kg)

Key features Long-legged, long-necked animal with short, inconspicuous tail; coat thick and woolly, usually beige to dark brown, sometimes pale with blotches; fur shorter and finer on head and legs; head small and sheeplike, with split upper lip; ears large, long, and mobile; feet smaller than those of camels, with 2 small hooves

Habits Feral and free-living animals live in groups dominated by single territorial male

Breeding Single calf born November–February after gestation period of 11–11.5 months. Weaned at 6–8 months; sexually mature at 1 year. May live at least 10 years in captivity, similar for feral populations

Voice Rumbling growls when angry or upset

Diet Grasses; leaves of other plants, trees, and shrubs

Habitat Grassland and scrub at high altitudes up to 13,000 ft (4,000 m)

Distribution Most live under domestication in Andes region of South America

Status Population: about 3,700,000; IUCN Extinct in the Wild. Domesticated

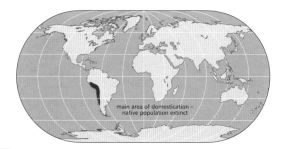

main area of domestication –
native population extinct

Moose

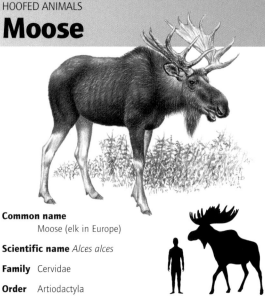

Common name
Moose (elk in Europe)

Scientific name *Alces alces*

Family Cervidae

Order Artiodactyla

Size Length head/body: 5–9.5 ft (1.6–2.9 m); tail length: 2.8–4 in (7–10 cm); height at shoulder: male 6–7.5 ft (1.8–2.3 m); female 5–5.6 ft (1.5–1.7 m)

Weight Male 700–1,760 lb (317–800 kg); female 605–825 lb (274–374 kg)

Key features Tall with long, thin legs; elongated head; fleshy "bell" hangs from throat; antlers may span 5 ft (1.5 m)

Habits Generally solitary, but herds may form in winter; often enters water, swims well

Breeding Single calf or twins (occasionally triplets) born May–June after gestation period of 240–250 days. Weaned at 5 months; sexually mature at 1 year. May live up to 27 years in captivity, 20 (females) or 15 (males) in the wild

Voice Deep lowing (males); muffled cough

Diet Tree shoots and twigs; large herbs, leaves, and aquatic plants in summer

Habitat Woodland and nearby open country

Distribution North America and northern Eurasia; introduced to New Zealand

Status Population: around 1 million in North America and 1 million in Eurasia; IUCN Lower Risk: near threatened (Siberian subspecies). Generally abundant and widespread

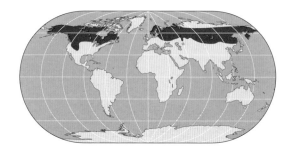

Reindeer/ Caribou

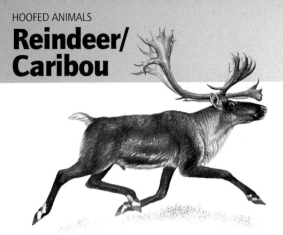

Common name Reindeer (Europe), caribou (North America)

Scientific name *Rangifer tarandus*

Family Cervidae

Order Artiodactyla

Size Length head/body: 6.2–7.2 ft (1.9–2.2 m); tail length: 4–6 in (10–15 cm); height at shoulder: 42–50 in (107–127 cm). Female generally 10–15% smaller

Weight 200–600 lb (91–272 kg)

Key features Large dark-brown deer, appears gray in winter; chest and legs darker than body, neck paler; patches of white on rump, tail, and above hooves; antlers in both sexes

Habits Lives in herds; moves seasonally to find food

Breeding Single calf, rarely twins, born May–June after gestation period of 210–240 days. Weaned at 1 month; sexually mature at 18–36 months. May live over 20 years in captivity, 15 in the wild (females), 10 (males)

Voice Series of grunting noises

Diet Lichens, sedges, grass, fungi; also browses leaves

Habitat Mainly Arctic tundra and forest edges

Distribution From Alaska through Canada to Greenland; Scandinavia through Europe and Russia to Sakhalin Island in North Pacific; introduced to Iceland, South Georgia, and other islands

Status Population: several million, including many semidomesticated animals in Europe; IUCN Endangered (subspecies *R. t. pearyi*)

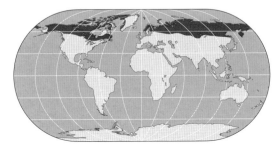

Red Deer

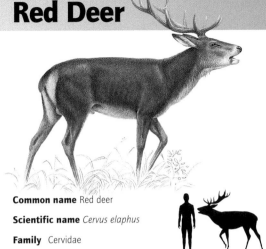

Common name Red deer

Scientific name *Cervus elaphus*

Family Cervidae

Order Artiodactyla

Size Length head/body: 5.6–8.5 ft (1.7–2.6 m); tail length: 6–8 in (15–20 cm); height at shoulder: about 47 in (120 cm)

Weight Male up to 560 lb (254 kg); female up to 330 lb (150 kg)

Key features Large brown deer with creamy-orange rump patch; no dark markings; branched antlers in male

Habits Mainly active at dawn and dusk; lives in herds; gathers in groups to breed in early fall

Breeding Single calf, occasionally twins, born after gestation period of 225–245 days. Weaned at 4–7 months; sexually mature at 1–3 years. May live 27 years in captivity, up to 25 in the wild, but usually only half that

Voice Males roar loudly on breeding grounds; females and calves make bleating noises

Diet Leaves and shoots from wide range of trees and shrubs; grass and sedges in winter

Habitat Prefers woodlands, but also found in parks and open hillsides; migrates above tree line in summer in Scandinavia

Distribution Widespread in Central Europe; scattered in Scandinavia, Mediterranean countries, Turkey, and east to Tibet; introduced in Australia, New Zealand, Texas, and South America

Status Population: abundant; generally increasing

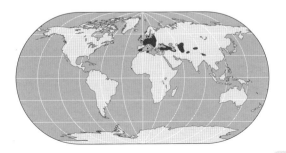

Giraffe

Common name Giraffe

Scientific name *Giraffa camelopardalis*

Family Giraffidae

Order Artiodactyla

Size Length head/body: 11.5–16 ft (3.5–4.8 m); tail length: 30–43 in (76–110 cm); height at shoulder: 8.2–12 ft (2.5–3.7 m)

Weight Male 1,760–4,250 lb (800–1,930 kg); female 1,210–2,600 lb (550–1,180 kg)

Key features Tall with long, flexible, maned neck and long, thin legs; body slopes down from shoulders to rump; both sexes have short horns; short coat has a pattern of chestnut-brown patches on creamy-white background

Habits Lives in loose groups; active both day and night; hardly sleeps

Breeding One calf born after gestation period of 453–464 days. Weaned at 12 months; females sexually mature at about 3.5 years, males at about 4.5 years. May live up to 36 years in captivity, 25 in the wild

Voice Grunts and snorts; calves bleat

Diet Leaves plucked from trees and shrubs, in particular from acacia, mimosa, and wild apricot trees

Habitat Open woodland and wooded grassland

Distribution Africa south of the Sahara, up to 6,560 ft (2,000 m) above sea level

Status Population: relatively abundant; IUCN Lower Risk: conservation dependent

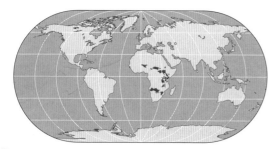

American Bison

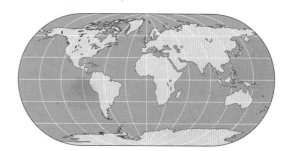

Common name American bison (buffalo)

Scientific name *Bison bison*

Family Bovidae

Order Artiodactyla

Size Length head/body: male 10–12 ft (3–3.8 m); female 7–10 ft (2.1–3.2 m); tail length: 17–35 in (43–90 cm); height at shoulder: up to 6.2 ft (1.9 m)

Weight Male 1,000–2,000 lb (454–907 kg); female 790–1,200 lb (358–544 kg)

Key features Large, oxlike animal with head held low and large hump over the shoulders; forelegs, neck, and shoulders covered in long, dark-brown hair; both sexes have horns

Habits Lives in large herds that migrate across open grasslands; feeds mostly early and late in day

Breeding Single calf born May–August after gestation period of 9–10 months. Weaned at about 6 months; sexually mature at 2–3 years. May live up to 40 years in captivity, up to 25 in the wild

Voice Snorts, grunts, and cowlike noises; bulls bellow and roar during the rut

Diet Mostly grass; also sedges, wild flowers, shrubs such as willow and sagebrush; lichens and mosses in winter

Habitat Prairies, sagebrush, and open wooded areas

Distribution Midwestern U.S. and Canada

Status Population: 200,000–500,000; IUCN Lower Risk: conservation dependent; Endangered (subspecies *B. b. athabascae*); CITES II

African Buffalo

Common name African buffalo

Scientific name *Syncerus caffer*

Family Bovidae

Order Artiodactyla

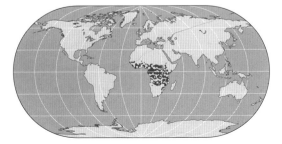

Size Length head/body: 8–11 ft (2.4–3.4 m); tail length: 30–43 in (75–110 cm); height at shoulder: 4.6–5.5 ft (1.4–1.7 m)

Weight 550–1,870 lb (250–848 kg). Male more heavily built than female

Key features Huge black or brown oxlike creature; hairy ears and massive horns that meet on top of the forehead to form a heavy "boss"; reddish forest form is smaller

Habits Lives in herds, sometimes of only a few animals, but many hundreds may congregate seasonally in good feeding areas

Breeding One calf normally produced every 2 years after gestation period of 11 months. Weaned at about 1 year; sexually mature at 3–5 years. May live over 29 years in captivity, 18 in the wild

Voice Generally silent

Diet Grass; wide variety of swamp vegetation

Habitat Savanna woodland and open grassy glades; usually near water and often wallows in mud; forest form lives under continuous tree cover

Distribution Widely dispersed across West, central, and East Africa south of Sahara

Status Population: probably at least 100,000; IUCN Lower Risk: conservation dependent. Common, but severely reduced in places due to disease, habitat loss, and hunting

Blue Wildebeest

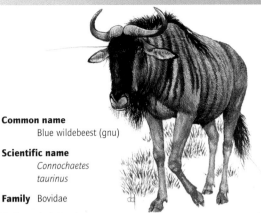

Common name Blue wildebeest (gnu)

Scientific name *Connochaetes taurinus*

Family Bovidae

Order Artiodactyla

Size Length head/body: 5.6–8 ft (1.7–2.4 m); tail length: 24–39 in (60–100 cm); height at shoulder: 47–59 in (120–150 cm). Female shorter than male

Weight Male 363–638 lb (165–290 kg); female 308–572 lb (140–260 kg)

Key features Large, cowlike antelope; humped shoulders and deep neck; dark mane with fringe under neck that varies in color with subspecies

Habits Gregarious: found in herds of up to 20 or 30; herds of thousands form during migrations; active in early morning and late afternoon

Breeding Single calf born each year after gestation period of 8–8.5 months. Weaned at 9–12 months; females sexually mature at about 16 months, males breed later due to competition with larger rivals. May live over 21 years in captivity, similar in the wild

Voice Loud snorts and low moaning grunts

Diet Fresh growth of several species of grass

Habitat Savanna woodland and grassy plains

Distribution Found in 2 main areas of Africa: from Kenya to Mozambique; also from Zambia into South Africa

Status Population: hundreds of thousands. A common animal

Impala

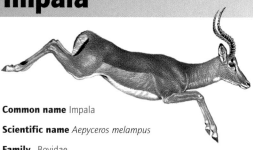

Common name Impala

Scientific name *Aepyceros melampus*

Family Bovidae

Order Artiodactyla

Size Length head/body: 47–63 in (120–160 cm); tail length: 12–18 in (30–45 cm); height at shoulder: 30–37 in (75–95 cm)

Weight Male 99–176 lb (45–80 kg); female 88–132 lb (40–60 kg)

Key features Medium-sized, sleek, and lightly built antelope; long, slender legs; characteristic tuft of black hair on lower and rear edge of hind legs; upper body bright reddish-brown, sides fawn, underparts white; black-tipped ears, white eyebrows; male bears slender, ridged horns

Habits Gregarious; acute senses: explosion of activity when disturbed; social structure differs with season; mostly active during day, although avoids midday sun; some nocturnal activity

Breeding Generally single calf born each year after gestation period of 6.5 months. Weaned at 5–7 months; females sexually mature at 18 months, males at 12–13 months. May live about 15 years in captivity, similar in the wild

Voice High-pitched bark and snorts when alarmed; males roar, snort, and growl during rut

Diet Grass; also leaves and shoots; fruit and seeds of trees and bushes

Habitat Open woodlands and grasslands

Distribution Central and southeastern Africa from Kenya to South Africa; small population in southwestern Africa around southern Angola

Status Population: many thousands; IUCN Lower Risk: conservation dependent

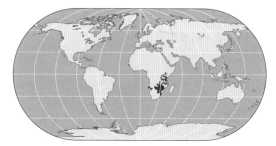

Thomson's Gazelle

Common name Thomson's gazelle (tommy)

Scientific name *Gazella thomsoni*

Family Bovidae

Order Artiodactyla

Size Length head/body: 31–47 in (80–120 cm); tail length: 6–11 in (15–27 cm); height at shoulder: 22–32 in (55–82 cm)

Weight Male 44–77 lb (20–35 kg); female 33–55 lb (15–25 kg)

Key features Small, slender antelope; pale-brown coat, white underside; bold black band from shoulder to flank; white ring around eyes and boldly striped face; ridged, parallel horns curve backward with tips turning forward

Habits Migratory; lives in herds of 60 or more, led by a single female; mature males often solitary and territorial

Breeding Generally single offspring born up to twice a year after gestation period of 5–6 months. Weaned at 4–5 months; females sexually mature at about 9 months, males first breed at about 3 years. May live about 16 years in captivity, 10 in the wild

Voice Feeble bleats and whistles

Diet Fresh green grass in rains; herbs, foliage, and seeds of shrubs in dry season

Habitat Open savanna grasslands

Distribution Suitable habitats in Tanzania and Kenya; also isolated population in southern Sudan

Status Population: probably many thousands; IUCN Lower Risk: conservation dependent

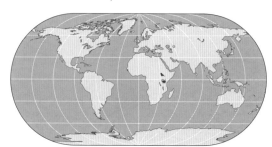

American Bighorn Sheep

Common name
American bighorn sheep

Scientific name *Ovis canadensis*

Family Bovidae

Order Artiodactyla

Size Length head/body: male 5.5-6.2 ft (1.7-1.9 m); female 4.9-5.2 ft (1.5-1.6 m); tail length: 3-5 in (7-12 cm); height at shoulder: 27.5-43 in (70-110 cm)

Weight Male 126-310 lb (57-140 kg); female 125-175 lb (57-80 kg)

Key features Brown body; white muzzle, underparts, and rump patch; brown horns—large and curled in rams, smaller and straighter in ewes

Habits Active by day; sociable: congregates in same-sex groups

Breeding Usually single lamb born after gestation period of about 175 days. Weaned around 4-5 months; females sexually mature at 4-5 years, males at 6-7 years. May live 24 years in captivity, 12 in the wild.

Voice Bleating in lambs; short, deep "baa" in adults

Diet Mainly grasses; also forbs and some shrubs

Habitat Semiopen rocky terrain; alpine to dry desert

Distribution Southwestern Canada to western U.S. and northern Mexico

Status Population: 65,000-68,000; IUCN Lower Risk: conservation dependent; CITES II. Hunting now controlled, but poaching continues in some areas

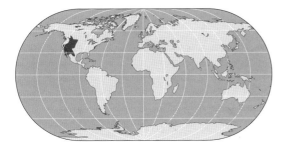

Pronghorn

Common name Pronghorn (antelope)

Scientific name *Antilocapra americana*

Family Antilocapridae

Order Artiodactyla

Size Length head/body: 46-52 in (116-133 cm); tail length: 4-5.5 in (10-14 cm); height at shoulder: about 34 in (87 cm)

Weight Male 92.5-130 lb (42-59 kg); female 90-110 lb (41-50 kg)

Key features Long-legged antelope with stocky body; upperparts pale brown, white belly, flanks, throat, and rump; males have black face mask; single forward-pointing prong

Habits Active during day, with short feeding bouts at night; lives in single-sex herds for most of year; some populations migratory

Breeding Usually twins born after gestation period of 251 days. Weaned at 4-5 months; females sexually mature at 15-16 months, males at 2-3 years but breed later. May live 12 years in captivity, 9-10 in the wild

Voice Grunts and snorts; lambs bleat, males roar

Diet Forbs, shrubs, grasses; often cacti and crops

Habitat Rolling grassland and bush; open conifer forests

Distribution Western U.S., Canada, parts of northern Mexico

Status Population: over 1 million; IUCN various subspecies listed as Critically Endangered, Endangered, and Lower risk: conservation dependent; CITES I. Species as a whole no longer threatened

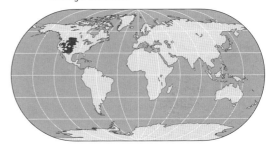

Springhare

Northern Pocket Gopher

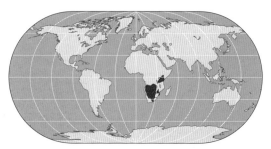

Common name Springhare (springhaas)

Scientific name *Pedetes capensis*

Family Pedetidae

Order Rodentia

Size Length head/body: 14–17 in (36–43 cm); tail length: 14.5–19 in (37–48 cm)

Weight 6.6–8.8 lb (3–4 kg)

Key features Kangaroolike rodent with very small forelimbs and long back feet; short snout; large eyes; big, leaf-shaped ears; fur thin and soft, reddish-brown to buff, paler on belly; end of tail has big black brush

Habits Generally nocturnal; digs burrows; lives alone but feeds in groups; hops on hind legs like a kangaroo

Breeding Three litters of 1 (occasionally 2) young born at any time of year after gestation period of 80 days. Weaned at 7 weeks; sexually mature at 2–3 years. May live up to 19 years in captivity, probably many fewer in the wild

Voice Soft grunts and high-pitched piping calls

Diet Roots, bulbs, and grasses; leaves and seeds of other plants, including crops; occasionally insects such as locusts and beetles

Habitat Desert and semidesert with dry sandy soils

Distribution Two populations: 1 in Kenya and Tanzania; the other in arid and semiarid parts of Angola, southern Democratic Republic of Congo, Namibia, South Africa, Botswana, Zimbabwe, and southern Mozambique

Status Population: unknown, probably tens of thousands; IUCN Vulnerable. Still abundant, but declining rapidly; hunted for food and as a crop pest

Common name Northern pocket gopher (western pocket gopher)

Scientific name *Thomomys talpoides*

Family Geomyidae

Order Rodentia

Size Length head/body: 5–7 in (12–19 cm); tail length: 1.5–3 in (4–8 cm)

Weight 2–6 oz (57–170 g). Male up to twice as heavy as female

Key features Robust body with short legs and large, long-clawed feet; tail short with naked tip; very thick neck and massive head, with small eyes and ears; lips close behind prominent incisor teeth; coat short and silky, any shade of brown from near-black to creamy white

Habits Solitary; aggressive; burrowing; mostly nocturnal

Breeding Single litter of 1–10 (usually 3–5) young born in spring after gestation period of 18 days. Weaned at 40 days; sexually mature at 1 year. May live up to 4 years in the wild, probably similar in captivity, although not normally kept for very long

Voice Generally silent

Diet Roots, bulbs, tubers, stems, and leaves of various plants, including many crops

Habitat Prairie grassland, forest, agricultural land, and anywhere else with soil suitable for burrowing

Distribution Southwestern Canada and western U.S.

Status Population: abundant. Some subspecies may be threatened by habitat loss

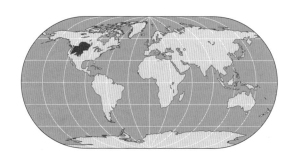

American Beaver

Common name
American beaver (Canadian beaver)

Scientific name *Castor canadensis*

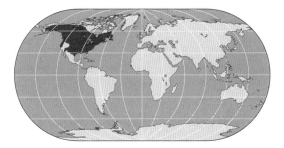

Family Castoridae

Order Rodentia

Size Length head/body: 31-47 in (80-120 cm); tail length: 10-20 in (25-50 cm)

Weight 24-66 lb (11-30 kg)

Key features Robust body with short legs; large, webbed hind feet; tail scaly, flattened, and paddlelike; small eyes and ears; coat dense and waterproof, light to rich dark brown

Habits Lives in small territorial colonies of related animals; semiaquatic; fells small trees to build lodges and dams that are of great importance to wetland ecosystem; largely nocturnal

Breeding Single litter of 1-9 (usually 2-4) young born in spring after gestation period of 100-110 days. Weaned at 3 months; sexually mature at 18-24 months. May live over 24 years in captivity, up to 24 in the wild

Voice Hisses and grunts; also announces presence by slapping tail on water surface

Diet Aquatic plants such as water lilies and leaves; also bark, twigs, roots, and other woody tissues of waterside trees and shrubs

Habitat Lakes and streams among light woodland

Distribution Canada, Alaska, and much of contiguous U.S.; introduced to parts of Finland

Status Population: 6-12 million. Abundant—recovered well after serious decline due to excessive fur trapping in 18th and 19th centuries; regulated hunting still takes place

Gray Squirrel

Common name Gray squirrel (American gray squirrel)

Scientific name *Sciurus carolinensis*

Family Sciuridae

Order Rodentia

Size Length head/body: 9-11 in (24-29 cm); tail length: 8-9 in (20-24 cm)

Weight 14-21 oz (400-600 g)

Key features Chunky squirrel with variable silvery to dark-gray fur, tinged with brown in summer; black individuals or subgroups also occur; tail bushy and fringed with white; ears rounded and without hairy tips

Habits Diurnal; tree-dwelling; also forages extensively on the ground; solitary, but nonterritorial; bold and inquisitive

Breeding One or 2 litters of 1-7 young born January–February and May–June after gestation period of 44-45 days. Weaned at 8 weeks; females sexually mature at 8 months, males at 10-11 months. May live up to 10 years in captivity, usually fewer in the wild

Voice Churring and chattering sounds; screams in distress

Diet Seeds and nuts, especially acorns; also buds, flowers, fruit, insects, and eggs

Habitat Mixed deciduous woodland

Distribution Southeastern Canada and eastern U.S.; introduced populations in Britain, Italy, and South Africa

Status Population: abundant

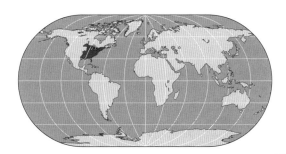

Eastern Chipmunk

Common name Eastern chipmunk

Scientific name *Tamias striatus*

Family Sciuridae

Order Rodentia

Size Length head/body: 5.5-7 in (14-17 cm); tail length: 3-5 in (8-12 cm)

Weight 3-5 oz (85-140 g)

Key features Large chipmunk with reddish-brown coat, fading to cream on belly, with 5 black stripes along back separated alternately by brown-and-white fur; large internal cheek pouches; bottlebrush tail covered in short hair; ears rounded, eyes large and bright; face also has striped markings

Habits Diurnal; solitary; territorial; digs extensive burrows—may stay there in winter, but does not hibernate

Breeding One or 2 litters of 1-9 (usually 3-5) young born in spring and summer after gestation period of 31 days. Weaned at 6 weeks; sexually mature at 10-12 months. May live up to 8 years in captivity, 3 in the wild

Voice High-pitched chirping calls

Diet Nuts, seeds, acorns, fungi, fruit, and crop plants; occasionally insects, birds' eggs, and baby mice

Habitat Lightly wooded land with warm, dry soils and rocky crevices in which to hide

Distribution Eastern U.S. and southeastern Canada

Status Population: abundant. Threatened by persecution and habitat loss in some agricultural areas

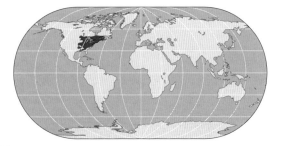

Black-Tailed Prairie Dog

Common name Black-tailed prairie dog (plains prairie dog)

Scientific name *Cynomys ludovicianus*

Family Sciuridae

Order Rodentia

Size Length head/body: 10-12 in (26-31 cm); tail length: 3-4 in (7-9.5 cm). Female about 10% smaller than male

Weight 20-53 oz (575-1,500 g)

Key features Sturdily built squirrel with short legs and short tail with black tip; coat buffy gray

Habits Diurnal and fossorial; highly social but also territorial; does not hibernate

Breeding Single litter of 1-8 (usually 3-5) young born in spring after gestation period of 34-37 days. Weaned at 5-7 weeks; sexually mature at 2 years. May live up to 8 years in captivity, 5 in the wild

Voice Various barks, squeaks, and soft churring sounds

Diet Grasses and herbs

Habitat Open short-grass plains and prairies; also pastureland

Distribution Great Plains of North America from southern Canada (Saskatchewan) to northern Mexico

Status Population: more than 1 million; IUCN Lower Risk: near threatened. Has declined due to habitat modification and persecution

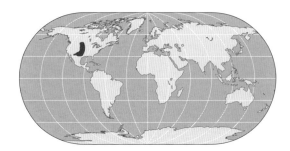

Southern Flying Squirrel

Common name Southern flying squirrel (eastern flying squirrel)

Scientific name *Glaucomys volans*

Family Sciuridae

Order Rodentia

Size Length head/body: 8-9 in (21-24 cm); tail length: 3-4 in (8-10 cm)

Weight 1.7-4 oz (50-120 g)

Key features Small silvery-gray squirrel with bushy but flattened tail and furry gliding membrane stretching from wrists to ankles; head large with big ears and huge black eyes

Habits Nocturnal, social, and gregarious; arboreal; hoards food—does not hibernate; "flies" by gliding on flaps of skin stretched between front and back limbs

Breeding One or 2 litters of 1-6 (usually 2-4) young born in spring and summer after gestation period of 40 days. Weaned at 8-9 weeks; sexually mature at 9 months. May live up to 14 years in captivity, fewer in the wild

Voice Chirping and squeaking calls, many of which are too high-pitched for humans to hear

Diet Nuts, acorns, bark, fungi, fruit, and lichen; occasionally eats insects and meat

Habitat Woodland

Distribution Southeastern Canada, eastern U.S., and Central America south to Honduras

Status Population: abundant. Has declined in some areas due to deforestation, but generally secure; may be responsible for the decline of the related but much rarer northern flying squirrel in some areas

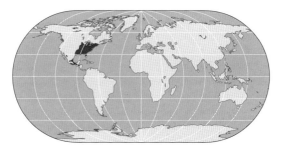

House Mouse

Common name House mouse

Scientific name *Mus musculus*

Family Muridae

Order Rodentia

Size Length head/body: 3-4.5 in (8-11 cm); tail length: 3-4 in (8-10 cm)

Weight 0.5-1 oz (14-28 g)

Key features Small, slim body; pointed face with large, sparsely haired ears; long, scaly pink tail; fur grayish-brown, often greasy and smelly

Habits Generally nocturnal; often aggressive; excellent climber, also swims well; lives wild and in association with people

Breeding Up to 14 litters of 4-10 young born at any time of year after gestation period of 19-21 days (more if female is suckling previous litter). Weaned at 3 weeks; sexually mature at 6 weeks. May live up to 6 years in captivity, 2 in the wild

Voice Squeaks

Diet Omnivorous: almost anything of plant or animal origin, including leather, wax, cloth, soap, and paper; also chews man-made materials such as plastics and synthetic fabrics

Habitat Farms, food supplies, fields, and houses

Distribution Almost worldwide

Status Population: billions. Less common than previously in many developed countries due to intensive pest control and mouse-proof buildings

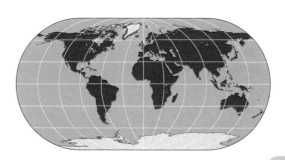

Brown Rat

Common name Brown rat (common rat, Norway rat)

Scientific name *Rattus norvegicus*

Family Muridae

Order Rodentia

Size Length head/body: 9–11 in (22–29 cm); tail length: 7–9 in (17–23 cm)

Weight 9–28 oz (255–790 g)

Key features Typical rat with short legs, longish fingers and toes, and pointed face; ears pink and prominent; scaly tail noticeably shorter than head and body; fur dull grayish-brown, fading to white or pale gray on belly

Habits Generally nocturnal; social; cautious at first but can become bold; climbs and swims well

Breeding Up to 12 litters of 1–22 (usually 8 or 9) young born at any time of year (but mostly in spring and summer) after gestation period of 21–26 days. Weaned at 3 weeks; sexually mature at 2–3 months. May live up to 6 years in captivity, 3 in the wild

Voice Loud squeaks when frightened or angry

Diet Anything edible, including fruit, grain, meat, eggs, wax, and soap; will catch and kill other small animals

Habitat Almost anywhere food can be found

Distribution Worldwide in association with humans; not normally in more sparsely populated areas of the world

Status Population: several billion

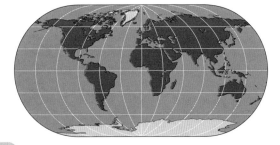

Golden Hamster

Common name Golden hamster (Syrian hamster)

Scientific name *Mesocricetus auratus*

Family Muridae

Order Rodentia

Size Length head/body: 6.5–7 in (17–18 cm); tail length: 0.5 in (1 cm)

Weight 3.5–4 oz (99–113 g)

Key features Short-tailed animal with sandy fur fading to white on belly; head broad with prominent rounded ears and huge cheek pouches; females have 12–16 mammae

Habits Mostly nocturnal; burrowing; socially aggressive; capable of hibernation

Breeding Three to 5 litters of 2–16 young born at any time of year (mostly spring and summer) after gestation period of 16–19 days. Weaned at 20 days; sexually mature at 8 weeks. May live 3 years in captivity, fewer in the wild

Voice Generally silent

Diet Very varied: includes seeds, shoots, fruit, and other plant material; also insects and other invertebrates and meat scavenged as carrion

Habitat Steppe and dry, rocky, scrubland

Distribution Aleppo region of northwestern Syria

Status Population: probably a few hundred in the wild; IUCN Endangered. Many thousands bred in captivity every year

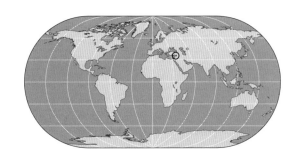

Norway Lemming

Common name
Norway lemming

Scientific name *Lemmus lemmus*

Family Muridae

Order Rodentia

Size Length head/body: 3-6 in (7-15.5 cm); tail length: about 0.5-1 in (1-2 cm)

Weight 0.4-5 oz (11-142 g)

Key features Rounded body and head; very short tail; thick coat creamy-yellow on underside, legs, and feet, but deep reddish-brown on back; darker on shoulders, head, and face; ears small and hidden in fur; eyes small and bright; thumb of each front foot bears large, flat snow claw

Habits Active at any time of day; does not hibernate; lives in burrows in ground or snow; swims well; aggressive and unsociable; overcrowded populations occasionally undertake mass migrations

Breeding Up to 6 litters of 1-13 (usually 5-8) young born in spring and summer (or every 21 days all year round under ideal conditions) after gestation period of 16-23 days. Weaned at 14-16 days; females sexually mature at 2-3 weeks, males at 3-4 weeks. May live up to 2 years, usually fewer, in the wild; not normally kept in captivity

Voice Various squeaks and whistles

Diet Mostly mosses; also leaves and shoots of grasses and sedges, lichen, fruit, and bark

Habitat Tundra

Distribution Norway, Sweden, Finland, and extreme northwestern Russia

Status Population: generally abundant but fluctuates wildly from year to year

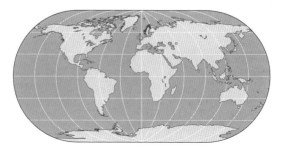

North American Porcupine

Common name North American porcupine (quillpig)

Scientific name *Erethizon dorsatum*

Family Erethizontidae

Order Rodentia

Size Length head/body: 25-34 in (64.5-86 cm); tail length: 5.5-12 in (14-30 cm)

Weight 7.7-40 lb (3.5-18 kg)

Key features Large rodent covered in stiff, brown to black fur; long, yellow spines on head, back, rump, flanks, and tail; feet have long, thick claws; short face with small, dark eyes and small ears hidden in hair

Habits Usually nocturnal; partially arboreal; lives alone or in small groups when breeding or sheltering in winter

Breeding Single young born April-June after 7.5 months' gestation. Weaned at 2-6 weeks; sexually mature at 2 years. May live 18 years in captivity, similar in the wild

Voice Grunts, growls, coughs, barks, and whines; also makes clattering sound with teeth

Diet Plant material, including leaves, shoots, buds, flowers, fruit, seeds, nuts, twigs, bark, wood; also gnaws bones

Habitat Mixed forest; also tundra, farmland, scrubland, and desert close to wooded areas

Distribution North America from Alaska throughout most of Canada and the continental U.S. south to northern Mexico and the Carolinas

Status Population: abundant

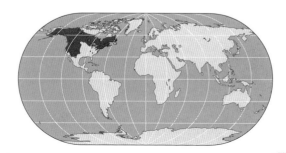

Guinea Pig

Coypu

Common name Coypu
(nutria, swamp beaver)

Scientific name *Myocastor coypus*

Family Myocastoridae

Order Rodentia

Size Length head/body: 17–25 in
(43–63 cm); tail length:
10–16.5 in (25–42 cm)

Weight 11–37.5 lb (5–17 kg)

Key features Large, ratlike animal with coarse, reddish-brown
coat and soft, velvety underfur; tail long, scaly, and
sparsely furred; head large with prominent orange
incisor teeth and small eyes and ears; hind feet webbed

Habits Active day and night; semiaquatic, excellent swimmer
and diver; lives in waterside burrows in pairs or small
family groups

Breeding Two to 3 litters of 1–13 (usually 4–6) young born in
spring and summer after gestation period of 4.5 months.
Weaned at 1–8 weeks; sexually mature at 3–7 months.
May live up to 7 years in captivity, rarely more than 4 in
the wild

Voice Grunts and growls; also squawks and grinds teeth

Diet Aquatic plants and nearby crops

Habitat Marshes, lakes, slow-flowing rivers, and streams

Distribution Native range covers southern South America,
including southern Brazil, Paraguay, Bolivia, and
Uruguay; introduced elsewhere

Status Population: abundant. Widely trapped for fur; now a
serious nuisance outside native range

Common name Guinea pig (domestic cavy)

Scientific name *Cavia porcellus*

Family Caviidae

Order Rodentia

Size Length head/body: 8–16 in
(20–40 cm)

Weight 1.1–3.3 lb (0.5–1.5 kg)

Key features Robust, ratlike body with short legs, no tail,
and large head; small ears and round eyes; coat
usually grayish-brown in feral forms, variable in
domestic varieties

Habits Nocturnal; social; timid; terrestrial; can swim well
when necessary

Breeding Several litters of 1–13 young born at any time of
year after gestation period of 63–68 days. Weaned at
3 weeks; sexually mature at 2 months. May live up to
8 years in captivity, probably fewer in the wild

Voice Conversational squeaks, chirps, and chattering

Diet All kinds of plant matter

Habitat Usually captive; feral animals live in grassland and
forest margins

Distribution Captive and feral only; farmed in Andean region
of South America

Status Population: abundant. Does not exist in original
wild state

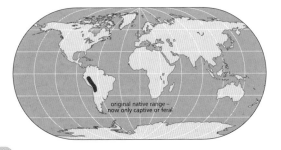

original native range –
now only captive or feral

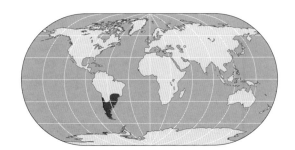

Capybara

Common name Capybara

Scientific name *Hydrochaeris hydrochaeris*

Family Hydrochaeridae

Order Rodentia

Size Length head/body:
42–53 in (106–135 cm)

Weight 77–145 lb (35–66 kg)

Key features Tall, barrel-bodied rodent with slender legs and sparse reddish-brown hair; no tail; front feet have 4 toes, hind feet 3; large head with rectangular profile and deep muzzle; small ears and eyes; male has lozenge-shaped gland on top of face

Habits Semiaquatic; social; colonial; usually active by day, but often nocturnal where disturbed

Breeding One (occasionally 2) litters of 1–8 (usually 3–5) young born at any time of year after gestation period of 150 days. Weaned almost immediately; sexually mature at 12 months. May live up to 12 years in captivity, 9 or 10 in the wild

Voice Whistles, grunts, purring and clicking sounds; also coughing barks

Diet Grasses and aquatic plants

Habitat Grassland and forest alongside rivers and pools

Distribution South America: south of Panama and east of Andes Mountains, including Colombia, Venezuela, Brazil, and Paraguay south as far as northeastern Argentina

Status Population: numerous, but total unknown; IUCN Lower Risk: conservation dependent. Declining in many areas

Naked Mole Rat

Common name Naked mole rat
(sand puppy)

Scientific name *Heterocephalus glaber*

Family Bathyergidae

Order Rodentia

Size Length head/body: 3–3.5 in
(8–9 cm); tail length: 1–2 in (3–5 cm)

Weight 1–2.8 oz (28–80 g)

Key features Small, naked rodent with short legs and tail; a few whiskers on face and body; prominent incisor teeth; tiny eyes and ears with no external ear flaps; large feet have 5 clawed toes

Habits Adapted to a life underground; colonial and highly social, with division of labor and suppression of breeding in subordinates; active mostly by day

Breeding Litters of 1–27 young born at any time of year after gestation period of 67 days. Weaned at 1 month; sexually mature at 7 months, but few animals have opportunity to breed. May live up to 25 years in captivity, probably similar in the wild

Voice Generally silent

Diet Plant roots and tubers

Habitat Lives underground in dry soils of desert and semidesert

Distribution East Africa, including Ethiopia, Somalia, and Kenya

Status Population: not known

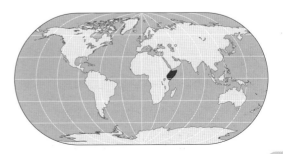

European Rabbit

Common name European rabbit (Old World rabbit, domestic rabbit)

Scientific name *Oryctolagus cuniculus*

Family Leporidae

Order Lagomorpha

Size Length head/body: 14–20 in (35–50 cm); tail length: 1.5–3 in (4–8 cm)

Weight 3–6.6 lb (1.3–3 kg)

Key features Stoutly built animal with powerful legs usually disguised by crouching stance; tail short and fluffy; head rounded with large, round eyes and long, erect oval ears; fur dense and soft, usually grayish-brown to black, paler on underside

Habits Mostly nocturnal but also active by day; lives in colonies in clustered burrows

Breeding Up to 7 litters of 1–9 (usually 5 or 6) young born in spring or summer after gestation period of 28–33 days. Weaned at 21 days; sexually mature at 3 months. May live up to 15 years in captivity, rarely more than 10 in the wild; most live fewer than a few months

Voice Usually silent; sharp squeals in pain or fright; drums feet to signal alarm

Diet Grass; also stems and leaves of other plants; nibbles bark in winter

Habitat Grassland

Distribution Much expanded by introductions over past 1,000 years; now occurs throughout Europe and northern Africa, also established in Australia and New Zealand

Status Population: extremely abundant, hundreds of millions. Widely persecuted as a pest

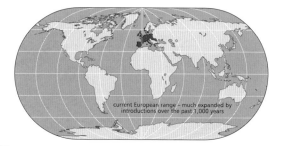

current European range – much expanded by introductions over the past 1,000 years

Black-Tailed Jackrabbit

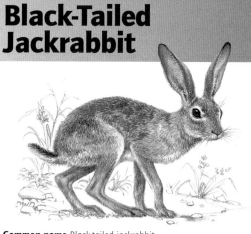

Common name Black-tailed jackrabbit

Scientific name *Lepus californicus*

Family Leporidae

Order Lagomorpha

Size Length head/body: 18.5–25 in (47–63 cm); tail length: up to 4 in (10 cm)

Weight 3.3–4.4 lb (1.5–4 g)

Key features Large hare with huge, erect black-tipped ears; legs long and slender; face has flat profile and large bulging eyes; fur grizzled gray-brown, paler below; dark dorsal stripe blends into black tail

Habits Active mainly in the evening; social; terrestrial, fast-moving, and nimble

Breeding Two to 6 litters of 1–6 (usually 3 or 4) young born at any time of year after gestation period of 41–47 days. Weaned at about 3 weeks; sexually mature at 7–8 months, but will often not breed until following year. May live up to 6 years in captivity, 5 in the wild

Voice Generally silent

Diet Grass and other plants of arid zones, including sagebrush, cactus, juniper, and mesquite; may raid cereal crops and orchards

Habitat Desert, prairie, and pasture in arid and semiarid areas

Distribution Southwestern United States and Mexico

Status Population: abundant, but fluctuates on 10-year cycle. Has increased in range and population since European settlement thanks to predator control

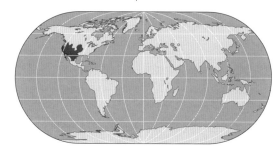

Arctic Hare

Common name Arctic hare (polar hare, Greenland hare)

Scientific name *Lepus arcticus*

Family Leporidae

Order Lagomorpha

Size Length head/body: 20–21 in (51–53 cm); tail length: 1.5–4 in (4.5–10 cm)

Weight 5.5–15 lb (2.5–7 kg)

Key features Gray or brown in summer with white tail; white all over in winter, except for tips of ears, which are black

Habits Usually solitary, but sometimes forms large groups; normally lives out in the open or among boulders

Breeding One litter of 2–8 young (average 5) born June or July after gestation period of 53 days. Weaned at about 8 or 9 weeks; sexually mature by following summer. May live about 7 years in the wild, not normally kept in captivity

Voice Normally silent

Diet Woody plants, moss, lichens, roots and flowers of willows; also some grasses

Habitat Tundra

Distribution Far north of Canada and Greenland south to Hudson Bay and Newfoundland

Status Population: total figure unknown. Common

American Pika

Common name American pika (common pika, Rocky Mountain pika, calling hare, mouse hare, coney)

Scientific name *Ochotona princeps*

Family Ochotonidae

Order Lagomorpha

Size Length head/body: 6.5–8.5 in (16–22 cm)

Weight 4–6.5 oz (110–180 g)

Key features Compact, rounded body with short neck and short legs; no visible tail; blunt head has short, round ears; fur is grayish-brown to buff with buffy underparts

Habits Solitary; aggressively territorial; terrestrial; diurnal; does not hibernate, but stores food for winter

Breeding Two litters of 1–6 (usually 3) young born spring and summer after gestation period of 30 days. Weaned at 30 days; sexually mature at 3 months. May live up to 7 years in captivity, rarely more than 5 in the wild

Voice Sharp alarm whistle and shrill courtship "song"; juveniles squeak

Diet Green plant material supplemented with stockpiled hay during winter

Habitat Boulder-strewn mountain slopes (talus) with patches of alpine grassland

Distribution Mountainous parts of western Canada and U.S. from British Columbia to central California and Colorado

Status Population: abundant

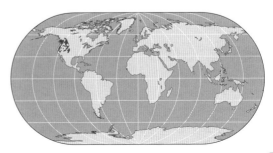

Western European Hedgehog

Common name Western European hedgehog (European hedgehog, urchin)

Scientific name *Erinaceus europaeus*

Family Erinaceidae

Order Insectivora

Size Length head/body: 6–10 in (16–26 cm); tail length: 0.5–1 in (1.5–3 cm)

Weight To 1–2.2 lb (0.5–0.9 kg), usually 17–28 oz (480–800 g)

Key features Spiny animal that rolls into a ball when alarmed; short tail; 5 long claws on each foot; general color grizzled brown and cream

Habits Nocturnal; normally lives alone; does not defend territory

Breeding Usually 4–6 (up to 8) young born in early summer after gestation period of 32–34 days (late litters born August–September). Weaned at 4–6 weeks; sexually mature at 1 year. May live up to 7 years in the wild, perhaps 10; fewer in captivity

Voice Snorts and grunts; piglike squeal if attacked

Diet Almost anything edible found at ground level, including beetles, worms, caterpillars, eggs, slugs, and occasional soft fruit

Habitat Farmland, short grass areas, hedges, woodlands, town parks, and gardens

Distribution Western Europe from Britain and southern Scandinavia to the Mediterranean east to Romania

Status Population: several million. Widespread and fairly abundant, especially in suburban areas

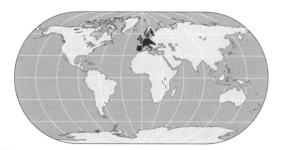

American Water Shrew

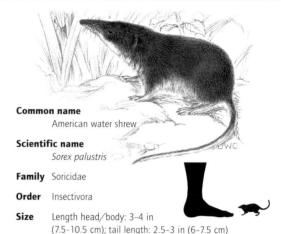

Common name American water shrew

Scientific name *Sorex palustris*

Family Soricidae

Order Insectivora

Size Length head/body: 3–4 in (7.5–10.5 cm); tail length: 2.5–3 in (6–7.5 cm)

Weight 0.3–0.5 oz (8.5–14 g)

Key features Quite large; blackish-gray coat sometimes becomes browner in summer; pale to dark-gray underside; 2-colored tail; distinctive fringe of stiff white hairs on sides of feet; tiny eyes and ears; red tips to teeth

Habits Solitary; active day and night but mostly just after sunset and before dawn; hunts in water

Breeding Litters of 3–10 young born late February–June after gestation period of about 21 days. Weaned at 28 days; sexually mature at 2 months in early-born young, 10 months in late-born young. May live about 18 months in captivity, similar in the wild

Voice High-pitched squeaks during territorial disputes

Diet Aquatic invertebrates such as caddisfly larvae and insect nymphs; occasionally small fish; on land takes flies, earthworms, and snails

Habitat Waterside habitats, especially in northern forests; prefers humid conditions

Distribution Canada; southeastern Alaska; mountain regions of U.S. into Utah and New Mexico, Sierra Nevada to California

Status Population: unknown, but likely to be millions. Widespread and abundant

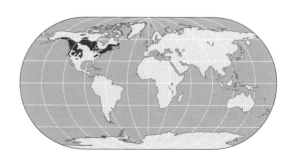

Giant Anteater

Common name Giant anteater

Scientific name *Myrmecophaga tridactyla*

Family Myrmecophagidae

Order Xenarthra

Size Length head/body: 39-51 in (100-130 cm); tail length: 25.5-35.5 in (65-90 cm)

Weight Male 53-86 lb (24-39 kg); female 48-77 lb (22-35 kg)

Key features Narrow, powerful body; small head with long, tapering snout; coat gray with black stripe from shoulders to chest and neck; hair coarse and stiff; long, bushy tail

Habits Solitary; generally diurnal; breaks into ant and termite nests

Breeding One young born in spring after gestation period of 190 days. Weaned at 6 months; sexually mature at 2 years. May live up to 26 years in captivity, unknown in the wild

Voice Generally silent

Diet Ants and termites; occasional beetle larvae and fruit

Habitat Grassland, swamp, and lowland tropical forest

Distribution Central America from southern Belize through South America to Northern Argentina

Status Population: unknown, but probably thousands; IUCN Vulnerable; CITES II

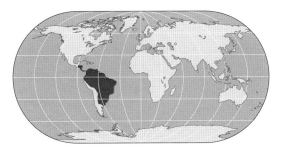

Three-Toed Sloth

Common name Three-toed sloth (brown-throated three-toed sloth)

Scientific name *Bradypus variegatus*

Family Bradypodidae

Order Xenarthra

Size Length head/body: 22-24 in (56-61 cm); tail length: 2.5-3 in (6-7 cm)

Weight 7.7-10 lb (3.5-4.5 kg)

Key features Long, shaggy fur; forelegs noticeably longer than hind legs; general color grayish-fawn, often with green tinge; small eyes; stumpy tail

Habits Hangs from branches, rarely descends to ground; stays in same tree for days at a time; moves only very slowly; active during day and at night

Breeding Single young born each year after gestation period of 5 months. Weaned at about 1 month, but stays with mother for further 4-6 months; sexually mature at about 2 years. May live over 20 years in the wild, not normally kept in captivity

Voice Normally silent

Diet Leaves collected from tree canopy

Habitat Lowland tropical forests

Distribution Honduras south to northern Argentina

Status Population: unknown, but probably declining. Close relative *B. torquatus* is classified Endangered by IUCN

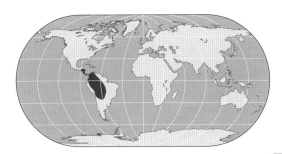

Nine-Banded Armadillo

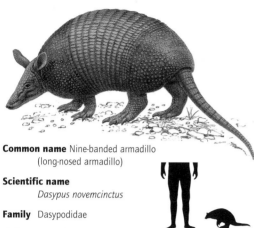

Common name Nine-banded armadillo
(long-nosed armadillo)

Scientific name
Dasypus novemcinctus

Family Dasypodidae

Order Xenarthra

Size Length head/body: 14.5–17 in (37–43 cm); tail length:
9.5–14.5 in (24–37 cm)

Weight 12–17 lb (5.5–7.5 kg). Female usually smaller than male

Key features Hard, shiny skin with scaly legs and tail; about
8–11 flexible bands around middle of body; long ears
and snout

Habits Generally nocturnal; shuffles around seeking food; lives
in shallow burrows

Breeding Four young born in spring after gestation period of
120 days (plus variable period of delayed implantation).
Weaned at 4–5 months; sexually mature at about 1 year.
May live at least 22 years in captivity, probably fewer in
the wild

Voice Constant, quiet grunting and sniffing when out foraging;
otherwise silent

Diet Mostly insects, especially termites; occasional worms,
snails, birds' eggs, and frogs

Habitat Short grass, forest floor, and farmland

Distribution Southern U.S. south to Uruguay and northern
Argentina and west to Peru; also Grenada and Trinidad
and Tobago in the West Indies

Status Population: abundant

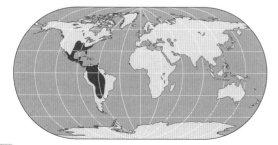

Aardvark

Common name Aardvark

Scientific name *Orycteropus afer*

Family Orycteropodidae

Order Tubulidentata

Size Length head/body: 41–51 in (105–130 cm); tail length:
18–25 in (45–63 cm)

Weight 88–143 lb (40–65 kg)

Key features Muscular, piglike animal with long nose, long
tail, and big ears; fur is coarse and sparse

Habits Solitary, shy, nocturnal, and rarely seen; digs
large burrows

Breeding Single young born after gestation period of about
7 months. Weaned at 6 months; sexually mature at
2 years. May live up to 18 years in captivity, probably
similar in the wild

Voice Occasional grunts

Diet Termites, ants, and insect larvae caught on long,
sticky tongue

Habitat Grassland, open woodland, and scrub where ants and
termites are abundant throughout year; avoids stony
soils and flooded areas

Distribution Patchily distributed throughout most of sub-
Saharan Africa

Status Population: unknown. Widespread, but exterminated
in many areas

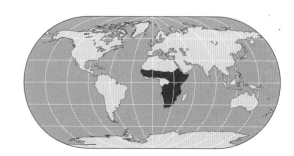

Indian Flying Fox

Common name Indian flying fox

Scientific name *Pteropus giganteus*

Family Pteropodidae

Order Chiroptera

Size Length head/body: 9–12 in (23–30 cm); forearm length: 6.5–7 in (16.5–18 cm); wingspan: 47–67 in (120–170 cm)

Weight Male 2–3.5 lb (0.9–1.6 kg); female 1.3–2.5 lb (0.6–1.1 kg)

Key features Large bat with a dark-brown body and black wings; male has light-yellow color on back of neck and shoulders

Habits Roosts in trees in large, mixed-sex groups; feeds at night on ripe fruit

Breeding Single young born usually in February after gestation period of 4–5 months. Weaned at 5 months; probably sexually mature at 1–2 years. May live up to 30 years in captivity, about 15 in the wild

Voice Variety of squawks and loud screams

Diet Ripe fruit, including mangoes, bananas, papayas, figs

Habitat Forests and swamps, always near a large body of water

Distribution Maldives, Pakistan, India, Sri Lanka, and Myanmar (Burma)

Status Population: unknown, but probably many thousands; CITES II

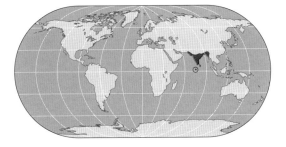

Vampire Bat

Common name Vampire bat

Scientific name *Desmodus rotundus*

Family Phyllostomidae

Order Chiroptera

Size Length head/body: 3–3.5 in (7–9 cm); forearm length: 2–2.5 in (5–6.3 cm); wingspan: about 20 in (50 cm)

Weight 0.5–1.8 oz (15–50 g)

Key features Dark-gray bat, paler on underside; snout flattened; vertical groove in lower lip

Habits Strictly nocturnal; usually lives in colonies of 20–100; roosts in caves, hollow trees, and old mines

Breeding Single young born once a year after gestation period of about 7 months. Weaned at 10 months; sexually mature at 1 year. May live at least 19.5 years in captivity, 15 in the wild

Voice Ultrasonic squeaks (too high-pitched for humans to hear); also aggressive squeaks if other vampires attempt to feed close by

Diet Feeds exclusively on blood, normally taken from mammals, including humans

Habitat Dry and wet areas of tropical and subtropical Central and South America

Distribution From Argentina and central Chile to northern Mexico; also Trinidad

Status Population unknown, but many thousands. Abundant, but probably declining

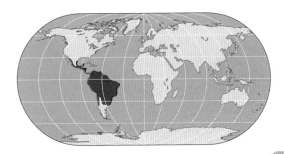

Little Brown Bat

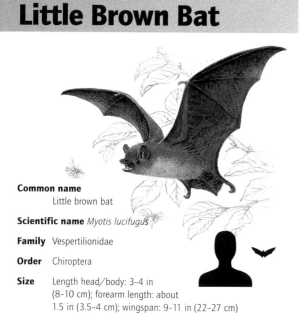

Common name
Little brown bat

Scientific name *Myotis lucifugus*

Family Vespertilionidae

Order Chiroptera

Size Length head/body: 3-4 in
(8-10 cm); forearm length: about
1.5 in (3.5-4 cm); wingspan: 9-11 in (22-27 cm)

Weight 0.25-0.45 oz (7-13 g)

Key features Small, fluttery bat with glossy fur of shades of
brown; underside paler; small, black ears with short,
rounded tragus; long hairs on toes

Habits Hunts insects over water; females gather in summer
nursery roosts, often in buildings; sexes hibernate
together in caves over winter

Breeding Single young born May-July after gestation period of
60 days. Weaned at 3 weeks; sexually mature in first
year in southern parts of range, second year farther
north. May live several years in captivity, 30 in the wild

Voice Short pulse echolocation calls 38-78 kHz, peaking at
about 40 kHz, too high-pitched for humans to hear

Diet Insects caught on wing, especially mosquitoes,
caddisflies, mayflies, and midges

Habitat Urban and forested areas; summer roosts in buildings or
under bridges, usually near water; hibernation roosts in
caves or mines

Distribution Alaska to Labrador and Newfoundland (Canada)
south to Distrito Federal (Mexico)

Status Population: probably several million. Not
seriously threatened

Fisherman Bat

Common name
Fisherman bat (bulldog bat)

Scientific name *Noctilio leporinus*

Family Noctilionidae

Order Chiroptera

Size Length head/body: 4-5 in (10-13 cm); forearm length:
3-4 in (8-10 cm); wingspan: 11-20 in (28-51 cm)

Weight 2.1-3.1 oz (60-88 g)

Key features Large bat with heavy doglike muzzle; nostrils
slightly tubular and downward pointing with "hare-lip"
fold of skin hanging below; large ears; tragus with
serrated edge; upperparts bright reddish-orange in
males, gray or dull brown in females

Habits Hunts surface-swimming fish and insects at night over
water; roosts in groups of 30 to several hundred; active
year-round

Breeding Single young born after 4 months' gestation. Weaned
at 3-4 months; sexually mature at about 1 year. May
live 11.5 years in captivity, probably more in the wild

Voice High-pitched chirping echolocation calls; lower-frequency
communication calls, including warning honk

Diet Mainly fish, but also crustaceans and insects

Habitat Near rivers, lakes, lagoons, or other water; roosts in
caves, rock clefts, and fissures

Distribution Southern Mexico to Guianas, Peru, southern Brazil,
northern Argentina, Trinidad, Greater and Lesser Antilles,
and southern Bahamas

Status Population: probably low thousands

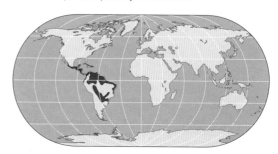

Virginia Opossum

Common name Virginia opossum
(common opossum, possum)

Scientific name *Didelphis virginiana*

Family Didelphidae

Order Didelphimorphia

Size Length head/body: 14-22 in (35-55 cm); tail length:
10-21 in (25-54 cm)

Weight 4.5-12 lb (2-5.5 kg)

Key features Cat-sized animal with short legs and long, naked
tail; pointed snout, large black eyes, and round, naked
ears; white-tipped guard hairs make coat appear shaggy;
hind feet have opposable first toe; female has up to 15
teats in well-developed pouch

Habits Mostly active at night; solitary; swims and climbs well

Breeding Up to 56 (usually about 21) young born after 13 days'
gestation. Young emerge from pouch at 70 days.
Weaned at 3-4 months; sexually mature at 6-8 months.
May live up to 5 years in captivity, 3 in the wild

Voice Clicking sounds; also growls, hisses, and screeches
when angry

Diet Small animals, including reptiles, mammals, and birds;
invertebrates such as insects; plant material, including
fruit and leaves; carrion; human refuse

Habitat Wooded areas or scrub, usually near water-courses or
close to swamps

Distribution Eastern and central U.S.; West Coast south through
Central America to Nicaragua

Status Population: abundant. Widespread; increasing in
numbers and range

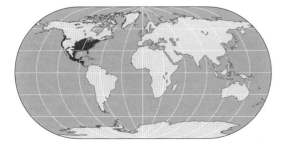

Numbat

Common name Numbat (banded anteater,
marsupial anteater)

Scientific name *Myrmecobius fasciatus*

Family Myrmecobiidae

Order Dasyuromorphia

Size Length head/body: 7-11 in (17-27 cm); tail length:
5-8 in (13-21 cm)

Weight 11-23 oz (300-650 g)

Key features Vaguely squirrel-like animal with long, tapering tail
and large feet with long claws; fur gray, tinged red on
upper back, paler beneath; rump distinctly marked with
white bars; muzzle long and pointed with small, black
nose and erect ears; eyes large with dark stripe running
through each; female has 4 teats, but no pouch

Habits Solitary; active during the day; lively, nimble creature
that climbs well

Breeding Two to 4 young born December–April after 14 days'
gestation. Young carried attached to teats for 4 months.
Weaned at 6 months; sexually mature from 9 months.
May live at least 6 years in captivity, 6 in the wild

Voice Soft snuffling sounds; hisses when disturbed

Diet Mostly termites and ants; some other insects

Habitat Dry, open woodlands and semidesert scrub

Distribution Southwestern parts of Western Australia

Status Population: unknown, but declining; IUCN Vulnerable.
Once found over much of southwestern and south-
central Australia; now restricted to a few small areas in
Western Australia; conservation has saved the species
from extinction

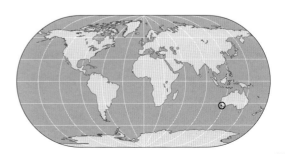

Thylacine

Common name Thylacine (Tasmanian wolf, Tasmanian tiger)

Scientific name *Thylacinus cynocephalus*

Family Thylacinidae

Order Dasyuromorphia

Size Length head/body: 33-51 in (85-130 cm); tail length: 15-26 in (38-65 cm); height at shoulder: 14-24 in (35-60 cm)

Weight 33-66 lb (15-30 kg)

Key features Superficially doglike animal, with a long body and long, rather stiff tail; coat short and coarse; tawny brown with dark stripes across the back, rump, and base of tail; female has simple, crescent-shaped, rear-opening pouch

Habits Active at night; usually solitary, although may have hunted cooperatively

Breeding Two to 4 young born after gestation period of about 1 month. Carried in pouch for 3 months. Weaned at about 9 months; sexual maturity unknown. (NB: all estimates from captive animals, situation in wild unknown). Lived up to 13 years in captivity, unknown in the wild

Voice Whines, growls, barks, and sharp yaps

Diet Mammals, including kangaroos, wallabies, smaller marsupials, and rodents; also birds

Habitat Forests

Distribution Widespread in Australia and New Guinea until about 3,000 years ago; restricted to Tasmania in historical times, but now extinct

Status Population: 0; IUCN Extinct

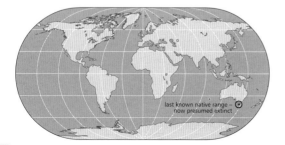

last known native range – now presumed extinct

Marsupial Mole

Common name Marsupial mole

Scientific name *Notoryctes typhlops*

Family Notoryctidae

Order Notoryctemorphia

Size Length head/body: 4-6 in (10-16 cm); tail length: 1 in (2.5 cm)

Weight 1.2-2.5 oz (34-70 g)

Key features Flat-bodied animal with pale golden fur and very short legs; front feet spadelike; no functional eyes; ear holes hidden in fur; nose has tough shield; tail is short and stubby; female has 2 teats in rear-opening pouch

Habits Solitary; "swims" through sand without creating permanent tunnels

Breeding Details not known

Voice Not known, but probably silent

Diet Insect grubs and other soil invertebrates; captive individuals are known to eat small reptiles

Habitat Desert

Distribution Central and northwestern Australia

Status Population: unknown; IUCN Endangered. Feared to be in decline

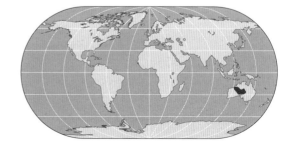

Red Kangaroo

Common name Red kangaroo

Scientific name *Macropus rufus*

Family Macropodidae

Order Diprotodontia

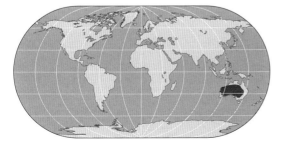

Size Length head/body: 29.5-63 in (75-160 cm); tail length: 25-47 in (64-120 cm); height: (upright) up to 6 ft (1.8 m)

Weight 37.5-198 lb (17-90 kg). Male may weigh up to twice as much as female

Key features Large kangaroo with rusty-red to blue-gray fur, paler on belly; female has 4 teats in a well-developed, forward-facing pouch

Habits Lives in loose groups; most active between dusk and dawn

Breeding Single young born at any time of year after gestation period of 33 days (plus up to 6 months delayed implantation). Incubated in pouch for 235 days. Weaned at 12 months; females sexually mature at 15-20 months, males at 20-24 months. May live more than 30 years in captivity, 27 in the wild

Voice Gruff coughing sounds

Diet Mainly grass; also leaves of other plants, including shrubs and trees

Habitat Scrub and open grassland, including arid and semiarid areas

Distribution Throughout central Australia; absent from the far north, eastern, and southeastern coasts, southwestern Australia, and Tasmania

Status Population: abundant. Remains common and widespread despite hunting and other control measures

Koala

Common name Koala (koala bear, native Australian bear)

Scientific name *Phascolarctos cinereus*

Family Phascolarctidae

Order Diprotodontia

Size Length head/body: 24-33 in (60-85 cm). Male larger than female; southern koalas larger than northern ones

Weight 9-33 lb (4-15 kg)

Key features Compact and teddy-bearlike with woolly, grayish-brown fur, paler on belly; large head with round, fluffy ears and large, black nose; tail stumpy; legs longer than they first appear, with 5 large claws on each foot; female has 2 teats in backward-opening pouch

Habits Solitary; nocturnal; arboreal; may come to the ground to cross open spaces

Breeding Single young (occasionally twins) born September to April (summer) after gestation period of 25-30 days. Leaves pouch after 5-7 months. Weaned at 6-12 months; sexually mature at 2 years. May live up to 20 years in captivity, 18 in the wild

Voice Screams, wheezing bellows, and loud wailing associated with courtship and aggression

Diet Leaves and bark of various species of eucalyptus trees

Habitat Eucalyptus forest and scrub

Distribution Eastern Australia

Status Population: about 40,000; IUCN Lower Risk: near threatened. Previously hunted for fur and threatened by loss of habitat; now protected and increasing

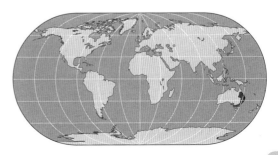

Common Wombat

Common name Common wombat

Scientific name *Vombatus ursinus*

Family Vombatidae

Order Diprotodontia

Size Length head/body: 27.5-47 in (70-120 cm); tail length: 1 in (2.5 cm)

Weight 33-77 lb (15-35 kg)

Key features Solid, short-legged, bearlike animal with very short tail; large head with short snout, large nose, and small ears; coat of coarse brown fur; long, powerful claws; female has 2 teats in rear-opening pouch

Habits Solitary; mostly active at night; digs large burrows

Breeding Single young (occasionally twins) mostly born in summer or fall after gestation period of 21 days. Spends a further 2-3 months in pouch. Weaned at 15 months; sexually mature at 2 years. May live up to 26 years in captivity, but fewer in the wild

Voice Grunts and abrupt coughing sounds

Diet Plant material, including leaves, stems, and roots; also fungi

Habitat Forests and scrub in rocky upland areas

Distribution Southeastern Australia and Tasmania

Status Population: many thousands; IUCN Vulnerable (Flinders Island subspecies). Has declined, but remains secure and common in parts of its geographical range away from human habitation

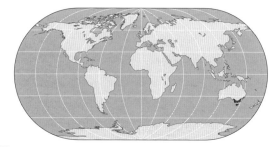

Honey Possum

Common name Honey possum (noolbenger)

Scientific name *Tarsipes rostratus*

Family Tarsipedidae

Order Diprotodontia

Size Length head/body: 1.5-4 in (4-9.5 cm); tail length: 2-4 in (4.5-11 cm)

Weight 0.2-0.6 oz (7-16 g)

Key features Tiny, mouselike marsupial with gray-brown fur marked with 3 dark stripes along the back; long snout and very long tail with hooked, prehensile tip; fingers are long with large, rounded tips and small nails; female has 4 teats in well-developed pouch

Habits Nocturnal; arboreal; excellent climber; often gregarious (lives in groups); goes torpid in cold weather

Breeding Two to 3 young born at any time of year after gestation period of 21-28 days (plus up to 2 months delayed development in the womb). Leaves pouch at about 4-6 weeks. Weaned at 10 weeks; sexually mature at 10 months. Rarely lives more than 1 year

Voice Normally silent

Diet Pollen and nectar

Habitat Trees and shrubs

Distribution Southwestern parts of Western Australia

Status Population: unknown but common. Not currently threatened, but may be at risk from habitat loss

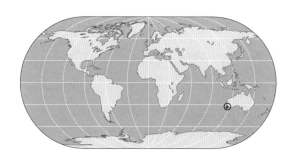

Duck-Billed Platypus

Common name Duck-billed platypus

Scientific name *Ornithorhynchus anatinus*

Family Ornithorhynchidae

Order Monotremata

Size Length head/body: 12–18 in (30–45 cm); tail length: 4–6 in (10–15 cm). Male usually larger than female

Weight 1–4.4 lb (0.5–2 kg)

Key features Flattened, torpedo-shaped animal with very short legs and large feet, each with 5 webbed toes; snout has soft, rubbery beak with nostrils on top; tail flat and paddlelike; body fur dark brown on back, paler below; male has sharp spurs on ankles

Habits Largely aquatic; most active around dusk and dawn; lives in burrows; generally solitary

Breeding One to 3 (usually 2) eggs laid after gestation period of 27 days. Young hatch 10 days later and are brooded for a further 4 months in nest burrow. Weaned at 4 months; sexually mature at 2 or 3 years. May live up to 21 years in captivity, 14 in the wild

Voice Usually silent; growls if disturbed or annoyed

Diet Small aquatic animals, especially crustaceans, insect larvae, worms, fish, and tadpoles

Habitat Freshwater streams and pools with suitable burrowing sites along their banks

Distribution Eastern Australia, including parts of Tasmania, New South Wales, Victoria, South Australia, and Queensland

Status Population: low thousands. Previously hunted for fur, now protected and doing well in most of its range

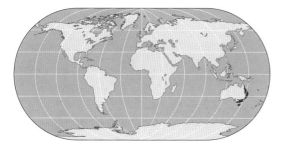

Short-Beaked Echidna

Common name Short-beaked echidna (short-nosed spiny anteater)

Scientific name *Tachyglossus aculeatus*

Family Tachyglossidae

Order Monotremata

Size Length head/body: 14–21 in (35–53 cm); tail length: 3.5 in (9 cm)

Weight 5.5–15.5 lb (2.5–7 kg)

Key features Stocky, short-legged animal with domed back covered in thick, dark-brown fur and long, black-tipped yellow spines; large feet have 5 toes with large, blunt claws; tail short; head small with long, whiskerless snout

Habits Solitary, but nonterritorial; usually nocturnal; may hibernate in parts of its range; terrestrial, but swims and climbs well; powerful digger

Breeding Single egg laid July–August after gestation period of 9–27 days. Incubated in pouchlike fold of skin on mother's belly; hatches after 10 days; spends further 8 weeks in pouch. Weaned at 6–7 months; sexually mature at 1–2 years. May live for over 50 years in captivity, rarely more than 20 in the wild

Voice Generally silent

Diet Ants and termites

Habitat Varied; forest and scrub, open rocky and sandy landscapes; also parks and gardens

Distribution Australia, including Tasmania; also New Guinea

Status Population: abundant. Common and widespread

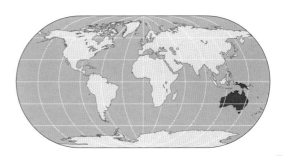

Glossary

Words in SMALL CAPITALS refer to other entries in the glossary.

Antler branched prongs on head of male deer, made of solid bone

Aquatic living in water

Arboreal living among the branches or leaves of trees

Baleen horny substance commonly known as whalebone and growing as plates in the mouth of certain whales; used like a sieve to extract plankton from seawater

Boreal forests Arctic forests (mostly conifers) at high latitudes

Browsing feeding on leaves of trees and shrubs

Canopy continuous (closed canopy) or broken (open canopy) layer in forests produced by the intermingling of branches

Carnivore meat-eating animal

Carrion dead animal matter used as a food source by SCAVENGERS

CITES Convention on International Trade in Endangered Species. Restricts international trade by licensing controls. Rare animals and plants listed in Appendices: I—endangered and most restricted trade; II—not endangered but could be if trade not restricted; III—least restricted trade

Coniferous forest evergreen forest of northern regions and mountainous areas dominated by pines, spruces, and cedars

Crepuscular active in twilight

Den a shelter, natural or constructed, used for sleeping, giving birth, and raising young

Diurnal active during the day

Dorsal relating to the back or spinal part of the body; usually the upper surface

Echolocation the process of perception based on reaction to the pattern of reflected sound waves (echos)

Estivation a period of inactivity or greatly decreased activity during hot or dry weather

Family technical term for group of closely related SPECIES that often also look similar. Zoological family names always end in "idae." Also, a social group within a species consisting of parents and their offspring

Feral domestic animals that have gone wild

Flukes flattened tail fins of whales

Forage to search for food, usually by BROWSING or GRAZING

Forb a herb other than grass

Generalist an animal that is capable of a wide range of activities, not specialized

Genus a group of closely related SPECIES. The plural is genera

Gestation the period of pregnancy between fertilization of the egg and birth of the young

Grazing feeding on grass

Gregarious living together in loose groups or herds

Guard hairs long, shiny hairs that project from UNDERFUR, particularly prominent in some AQUATIC rodents and CARNIVORES

Harem a group of females living in the same TERRITORY and consorting with a single male

Herbivore plant-eating animal

Hibernation a period of inactivity in winter, with lowered body temperature to save energy

Home range the area that an animal uses in the course of its normal periods of activity

Insectivores animals that feed on insects and similar small prey. Also a group name for animals such as hedgehogs, shrews, and moles

Invertebrates animals that have no backbone (or other true bones) inside their body, e.g., mollusks, insects, jellyfish, and crabs

IUCN International Union for the Conservation of Nature, responsible for assigning animals and plants to internationally agreed categories of rarity. (See table below.)

Juvenile young animal that has not yet reached breeding age

Mammae See MAMMARY GLANDS

Mammary glands characteristic of mammals, glands for producing milk

Mangroves woody shrubs and trees adapted to living along muddy coasts in the tropics

Molt process in which mammals shed hair, usually seasonal

Monogamous animals that have only one mate at a time

Monotreme egg-laying mammal, e.g., platypus, echidna

Montane in a mountain environment

Musk a substance with a penetrating odor produced in a sac beneath the abdominal skin of certain animals

Muzzle the projecting jaws and nose of an animal; snout

Nocturnal active at night

Nomadic animals that have no fixed home, but wander continuously

Nose-leaf fleshy structures around the face of bats; help focus ULTRASOUNDS used for ECHOLOCATION

Omnivore an animal that eats almost anything, meat or vegetable

Opportunistic taking advantage of every opportunity that arises; flexible behavior

Opposable fingers or toes that can be brought to bear against others on the same hand or foot in order to grip objects

Order a subdivision of a class of animals consisting of a series of related animal FAMILIES

Pair bond behavior that keeps a male and a female together beyond the time it takes to mate

Parasite animal or plant that lives on or in body of another

Population a distinct group of animals of the same SPECIES or all the animals of that species

Precocious when offspring develop early for their age

Predator an animal that kills live prey for food

Prehensile grasping tail or fingers

Pride SOCIAL group of lions

Primate a group of mammals that includes monkeys, apes, and humans

IUCN CATEGORIES

EX Extinct, when there is no reasonable doubt that the last individual of the species has died.

EW Extinct in the Wild, when a species is known only to survive in captivity or as a naturalized population well outside the past range.

CR Critically Endangered, when a species is facing an extremely high risk of extinction in the wild in the immediate future.

EN Endangered, when a species is facing a very high risk of extinction in the wild in the near future.

VU Vulnerable, when a species is facing a high risk of extinction in the wild in the medium-term future.

LR Lower Risk, when a species has been evaluated and does not satisfy the criteria for CR, EN, or VU.

DD Data Deficient, when there is not enough information about a species to assess the risk of extinction.

NE Not Evaluated, species that have not been assessed by the IUCN criteria.

Further Reading

Promiscuous mating often with many mates, not just one

Pup a young seal or sea lion

Range the total geographical area over which a SPECIES is distributed

Retractile capable of being withdrawn, as in the claws of typical cats, which can be folded back into the paws to protect from damage when walking

Riparian living beside rivers and lakes

Roost place that a bat or a bird regularly uses for sleeping

Ruminant animals that eat vegetation and later bring it back from the stomach to chew again ("chewing the cud" or "rumination") to assist its digestion by microbes in the stomach

Rut annually recurring state of sexual excitement in male deer (and other mammals); also describes the period during which this occurs

Savanna tropical grasslands with scattered trees and low rainfall, usually in warm areas

Scavenger animal that feeds on dead animals or plants that it has not hunted or collected itself

Scrotum bag of skin within which the male testicles are located

Scrub vegetation that is dominated by shrubs—woody plants usually with more than one stem

Secondary forest trees that have been planted or grown up on ground that has been cleared

Sexually mature having reached full reproductive development

Social living together in colonies

Solitary living alone or undertaking tasks alone

Species a group of animals that look similar and can breed to produce fertile offspring

Spy-hopping when a whale raises its head vertically out of the water to look around

Steppe open grassland in parts of the world where the climate is too harsh for trees to grow

Sub-Saharan all parts of Africa lying south of the Sahara Desert

Subspecies a locally distinct group of animals that differ slightly from normal appearance of SPECIES; often called a race

Temperate associated with a moderate climate

Terrestrial living on land

Territory an area that one or more animals defend against other members of the same SPECIES; these animals are territorial

Tropics permanently warm zone of the earth's surface centered on the equator, lying between the Tropic of Capricorn and Tropic of Cancer

Tundra open grassy or shrub-covered lands of the far north

Ultrasounds sounds that are too high-pitched for humans to hear

Underfur fine hairs forming a dense, woolly mass close to the skin and underneath the outer coat of stiff hairs in mammals

Ungulate hoofed animals such as pigs, deer, cattle, and horses; mostly HERBIVORES

Byers, J. A., *American Pronghorn*, University of Chicago Press, Chicago, IL, 1997.

Fossey, D., *Gorillas in the Mist*, Houghton Mifflin, New York, NY, 2000.

Gittelman, J. L., Carnivore Behavior, Ecology, and Evolution, Cornell University Press, Ithaca, NY, 1996.

Kingdon, J., *The Kingdon Field Guide to African Mammals*, Academic Press, San Diego, CA, 1997.

MacDonald, D., *The Encyclopedia of Mammals*, Facts On File, New York, NY, 2001.

Morria, P., and A-J. Beer, *World of Animals: Mammals* (Vols. 1–10), Grolier, Danbury, CT, 2003.

Nowak, R. M., *Walker's Bats of the World*, Johns Hopkins University Press, Baltimore, MD, 1995.

Perrin, W., *Encyclopedia of Marine Mammals*, Academic Press, New York, NY, 2002.

Rowe, N., *The Pictorial Guide to the Living Primates*, Pogonias Press, East Hampton, NY, 1996.

Steele, M., and J. L. Koprowski, *North American Tree Squirrels*, Smithsonian Institution Press, Washington, DC, 2001.

Strahan, R., *The Mammals of Australia*, Reed New Holland, Australia, 1998.

Sunquist, M., and F. Sunquist, *Wildcats of the World*, Chicago University Press, Chicago, IL, 2002.

Whitaker, J. O., *National Audubon Society Field Guide to North American Mammals*, Alfred A. Knopf, New York, NY, 1996.

Wilson, D. E., *The Smithsonian Book of North American Mammals*, Smithsonian Institution Press, Washington, DC, 1999.

Wilson, D. E., and D. M. Reeder, *Mammal Species of the World. A Taxonomic and Geographical Reference*, Smithsonian Institution Press, Washington, DC, 1999.

Useful Web Sites

http://www.acsonline.org
American Cetacean Society. Supports and reports research and conservation of whales, dolphins, and porpoises.

http://www.awf.org/wildlives/
An African Wildlife Foundation Web site.

http://www.batcon.org
Web site of Bat Conservation International.

http://www.carnivoreconservation.org/
News, links, recent books, etc., on carnivore ecology and conservation.

http://www.cites.org/
IUCN and CITES listings. Search for animals by scientific name, order, family, genus, species, or common name. Location by country and explanation of reasons for listings.

http://endangered.fws.gov
Information about threatened animals and plants from the U.S. Fish and Wildlife Service.

http://www.iucn.org
Details of species and their status; listings by the International Union for the Conservation of Nature. Also lists IUCN publications.

http://www.nccnsw.org.au
Web site for threatened Australian species.

http://www.panda.org
Web site of the World Wide Fund for Nature (WWF). Includes newsroom, press releases, government reports, and campaigns.

http://www.primates.org
General information and links on primates.

Index

Bold names, e.g., **aardvark**, are entry headings. Bold numbers indicate an animal that is the main subject of the illustrated entry. Italic numbers, e.g., *4*, point to other illustrations.